DAZZLING
bead
&
wire
CRAFTS

DAZZLING
bead
& wire
CRAFTS

Mickey Baskett

STERLING

New York / London
www.sterlingpublishing.com

Prolific Impressions Production Staff:
Editor in Chief: Mickey Baskett
Copy Editor: Phyllis Mueller
Graphics: Dianne Miller, Karen Turpin
Styling: Lenos Key
Photography: Jerry Mucklow
Administration: Jim Baskett

Every effort has been made to insure that the information presented is accurate. Since we have no control over physical conditions, individual skills, or chosen tools and products, the publisher disclaims any liability for injuries, losses, untoward results, or any other damages which may result from the use of the information in this book. Thoroughly read the instructions for all products used to complete the projects in this book, paying particular attention to all cautions and warnings shown for that product to ensure their proper and safe use.

Library of Congress Cataloging-in-Publication Data
Baskett, Mickey.
    Dazzling bead & wire crafts / Mickey Baskett.
        p. cm.
    Includes index.
    ISBN 1-4027-1445-9
    1. Beadwork. 2. Wire craft. I. Title: Dazzling bead and wire crafts. II. Title.
    TT860.B3336 2005
    745.58'2--dc22

                                                                    2005010483

10 9 8 7 6 5 4 3 2 1
Published by Sterling Publishing Co., Inc.
387 Park Avenue South, New York, N.Y. 10016
© 2005 by Prolific Impressions, Inc.
Produced by Prolific Impressions, Inc.
160 South Candler St., Decatur, GA 30030
Distributed in Canada by Sterling Publishing
c/o Canadian Manda Group, 165 Dufferin Street
Toronto, Ontario, Canada M6K 3H6
Distributed in the United Kingdom by GMC Distribution Services
Castle Place, 166 High Street, Lewes, East Sussex, England BN7 1XU
Distributed in Australia by Capricorn Link (Australia) Pty. Ltd.
P.O. Box 704, Windsor, NSW 2756 Australia

Printed in China
All rights reserved

Sterling ISBN-13: 978-1-4027-1445-0 Hardcover
        ISBN-10: 1-4027-1445-9
        ISBN-13: 978-1-4027-5204-9 Paperback
        ISBN-10: 1-4027-5204-0
For information about custom editions, special sales, premium and corporate purchases, please contact Sterling Special Sales Department at 800-805-5489 or specialsales@sterlingpub.com.

Acknowledgements:

Thank you to the following manufacturers for supplying products to create the projects in this book.

AMACO® (American Art Clay Co., Inc.), for polymer clay, Ph:† (800) 374-1600, http://www.amaco.com

Beadalon®, for beading wire, 800-824-WIRE, www.beadalon.com

The Beadery®, for beads, 401-539-2432, www.thebeadery.com

Halcraft USA, Inc., for Curiously Sticky Tape and glass marble, www.halcraft.com

Hampton Art, LLC, for rubber stamps, 19 Industrial Blvd, Medford, NY 11763, www.hamptonart.com

Judy's Stone House Designs, for wooden purse box, 970-622-9717, E-mail: JudysSHD@aol.com, www.JudysStoneHouseDesigns.com

Plaid Enterprises, Inc. / All Night Media for decoupage finish and rubber stamps, 678- 291-8100, www.plaidonline.com

Tandy Leather Company/The Leather Factory®, for leather, 1-800-890-1611 or 1-877-LEATHER, www.tandyleather.com

Tsukineko, Inc., stamping pigment ink, 425-883-7733, www.tsukineko.com

Table of

Contents

Beads and wire are perennial favorites for crafters - their many forms dazzle us by the sheer power of their beauty and versatility, and they can be combined in almost endless variation, delighting the eye and the imagination.

In this book, we continue our exploration of the wonderful world of beads and wire with more than 50 projects for all tastes and levels of expertise, from simple bent wire shapes and stringing techniques to creating wire filigree on a jig, bead making with polymer clay, and creating mosaics with beads and dimensional paint.

We begin with a section of information about supplies and tools that will help you get started. Then we move on to a varied and interesting collection of gorgeous jewelry - bracelets, necklaces, earrings - in classic and contemporary looks and fashionable accessories, including purses, a headband, and a pouch.

For the home, there are fun and fanciful pieces and ideas for embellishing furnishings and picture frames, journals to hold your thoughts and tins to hold your treasures, and imaginative, simple embellishments for the table. Photographs, step-by-step instructions, numerous illustrations, and patterns are presented in the individual project instructions.

I thank the designers who created these projects - Kathi Bailey, Patty Cox, Lisa Galvin, Cindy Gorder, Barbara Mansfield, Dena Mansfield, Ann Mitchell, and Karen Mitchell - for reminding us there are always new ideas to explore and experience when we begin with wire and beads.

Wire

Wire is the generic name given to pliable metallic strands that are made in a variety of thicknesses and lengths. Two basic characteristics distinguish one kind of wire from another: the type of metal used and the thickness, usually referred to as the gauge or diameter.

The type of metal a wire is made of gives the wire its color, and wire is often referred to by the names of three metallic "colors" - gold, silver, and copper. **Gold-colored wire** can be made of gold, brass, or bronze. **Silver-colored wire** can be made of silver, steel, aluminum, or tin-coated copper. **Copper-colored wire** is made of copper or copper plus another metal. The color of wire can be altered with spray paint, acrylic craft paint, or rub-on metallic wax. Wire also can be purchased in colors.

Commercially, wire is used to impart structure and conduct electricity, so it's not surprising that it's sold in hardware and building supply stores and electrical supply houses. You'll also find wire for sale in art supply stores, in crafts stores, and in stores that sell supplies for jewelry making, and from mail order catalogs.

Armature wire

Solder wire

Most any type of wire will work for the projects in this book. Just be sure to use the thickness (gauge) of wire listed in the supplies to get the same results as shown. It is best to use a wire that is non-corrosive so that your projects will have a long life.

Also consider the memory qualities of the wire you use. Some wire keeps its shape better than others. For example, armature wire is very pliable and will not keep its shape under pressure. If you are making a hanging candle holder, you want a stiff wire that holds the shape in which it is bent.

About Wire Gauges

The higher the number of the gauge, the thinner the wire; e.g., 24 gauge wire is thinner than 16 gauge wire. The "Supplies" sections of the projects in this book list the type of metal and the thickness or gauge of wire to use.

Types of Wire
• ARMATURE WIRE

A non-corrosive aluminum alloy wire, **armature wire** is easy to bend and doesn't tarnish. It is used by clay sculptors to build their armatures - the wire framework sculptures are built on. It is usually 1/8" or 1/4" thick or can be found by gauge measurement. You'll find it in stores that sell art and craft supplies. This is the wire that is used most for the projects in this book. Armature wire is great to use for projects where the wire is glued in place or wrapped around something stable.

• BUSS WIRE

Buss wire is tin-coated copper wire used as an uninsulated conductor of electricity. Shinier than aluminum wire and inexpensive, buss wire is silver in color and often used for making jewelry. It's available in various gauges. Look for it at hardware stores and electrical supply houses.

Beading wire, thin gauge wire, aluminum wire

Buss wire

• ALUMINUM WIRE

Soft and flexible, **aluminum wire** is silver in color and has a dull finish. It won't rust and is often used for constructing electric fences. It's available at building supply and hardware stores. It is a stiffer wire and holds its shape quite nicely.

• SOLDER WIRE

Used by plumbers to solder pipe, **solder wire** is soft, silver-colored, and easy to bend. It comes on a spool and is sold by the pound. Be sure to buy solder that is solid core and lead-free. It can be found at hardware and building supply stores. This wire is good to use for projects where the wire shapes will be glued on a surface or wrapped around something.

• THIN GAUGE WIRE

Bought by the spool or the package, **thin wire** - from 16 to 28 gauge - can be made of a variety of metals, including sterling silver, brass, gold, copper, steel, and galvanized tin. You can find it in hobby shops, crafts stores, hardware stores, and stores that sell supplies for jewelry making.

• COLORED WIRE

Colored wire is aluminum wire that has had color incorporated into the wire by a process known as anodizing. The colors are vibrant and permanent.

Colored-coated wire is metal wire coated with a thin layer of colored vinyl or paint.

• BEADING WIRE

Beading wire is manufactured specifically for beading. Beaded jewelry is often made on a special plastic-coated wire that comes in a variety of thicknesses. It is sold in stores that sell jewelry-making supplies.

Colored wire

Beads

Seed beads

Faceted beads

Beads are made all over the world and can be found at crafts stores and the notions departments of variety and department stores. There are literally hundreds of shapes, sizes, and colors from which to choose. Beads are made of a variety of materials, including glass, wood, ceramic, metal, acrylic, semi-precious stones, clay, and natural minerals. They are classified according to material, shape, and size. Most beads have holes in them for stringing or threading on wire. Their sizes generally are measured in millimeters (mm).

Bugle beads

Types of Beads

• BUGLE BEADS

Bugle beads are tubular-shaped glass beads. They are most frequently seen in jewelry designs and beaded clothing.

• SEED BEADS

Seed beads are small, rounded glass beads that are oblate in shape (fatter in diameter than they are long). They are also called **E beads** or **rocaille beads**. E beads are usually larger than seed beads.

• FACETED BEADS

Faceted beads are made of molded glass or plastic. They have flattened, cut, ground, or polished reflective surfaces (called facets). They usually are transparent.

• STONES, CABOCHONS & MARBLES

Stones and **cabochons** don't have holes for stringing or threading, so when used with wire, they are secured by wrapping with wire or gluing in place. Stones may be of glass, natural minerals, acrylic, or semi-precious stones and generally have irregular shapes. Cabochons are glass, acrylic, or semi-precious stones that are flat on one side, making them ideal for decorating flat surfaces. They can be tear-drop shaped, round, or oval. Also available are **flat-backed marbles** that can be glued or wired in place.

Cabochons and stones

• LAMPWORK BEADS

Lampwork beads are individually handcrafted glass beads that are made from glass rods that are melted with a torch. The hot glass is wrapped around a wire that, when removed, forms the bead's hole. The bead is heated in a kiln and allowed to cool slowly (this process is known as annealing). Lampwork beads are usually one of a kind and used as focal beads in designs.

Jewelry Findings

Jewelry findings are the metal items that transform wire and beads into jewelry. You will need the following:

Clasps: These come in a wide variety of shapes, sizes, and designs. Choose the type they you like the best. You will find *barrel clasps, spring lock clasps, toggle clasps,* and *fish hook/box clasps. Magnetic claps* contain tiny magnets that hold together when they touch.

Jump rings are small metal rings that are used to attach one finding to another such as to attach an eyepin to an earring back. They are split so that they can be pried open and shut for use.

Earring findings come in both pierced and unpierced varieties. Pierced backs fall into two categories: *hooks* and *posts.* Unpierced backs are available in *screw-on* and *clip-on.*

Jewelry findings

Stick pins and pin backs are attached to your jewelry design to transform it into a pin.

Headpins are earring findings used to construct drop earrings. They come in a variety of lengths. Beads are threaded onto the pin then attached to an earring back. The headpin looks like a straight pin without a point at the tip.

Eyepins have a loop on the end and are used in the same manner as headpins.

Crimp beads are used to secure the wire loops that connect fasteners or to permanently join to wires when you're not using a clasp (on a necklace that slips over the head, for example). They are made of very soft metal; squeeze them with pliers (crimp) when in position and they will be permanently shut.

Glues

Several types of glue are used in wire projects. When using glues, be cautious! Many glues emit fumes as they dry. Always read the label and follow the manufacturer's precautions and instructions. Work in a ventilated area and avoid contact with your skin.

Jewelry glue is a clear-drying glue made specifically for gluing metal and stones. Find it at crafts stores and stores that sell jewelry-making supplies.

Metal glue is just that - a glue that's meant to adhere metal to metal. Find it at crafts and hardware stores.

Household cement or **multi-purpose adhesive** is general purpose glue sold under a variety of trade names. It can be used for metal, china, glass, and paper. It is a clear glue. It's available at crafts and hardware stores.

Epoxy comes in two containers - one contains a resin, the other a hardener. When mixed, their chemical action creates a strong, clear bond. You'll find epoxy at crafts and hardware stores.

Silicone glue will adhere metal to metal or beads to metal. Because it is thick and messy, silicone glue is better applied with a toothpick or other instrument rather than squeezing it directly from the tube onto an object.

Tools & Equipment

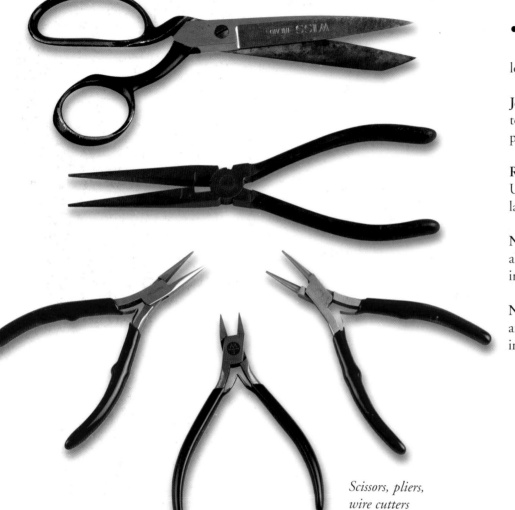

• PLIERS

Pliers are used for bending, twisting, looping, and coiling wire.

Jewelry making pliers are the best type to use when working with delicate projects and materials.

Roundnose pliers have rounded ends. Use smaller ones for delicate work and larger ones to make bigger loops.

Needlenose pliers or flatnose pliers, also called "snipe nose pliers," have flat inner surfaces and pointed ends.

Nylon-jaw pliers and **nylon-nose pliers** are used for flattening and manipulating wire beads without marring.

*Scissors, pliers,
wire cutters*

• CUTTERS

Available in a wide range of sizes, **wire cutters** are tools used for cutting wire. Thicker, lower gauge wire requires sturdy cutters. Very thin wire can be cut with smaller jewelry-making wire cutters. Very thin wire can be cut with **scissors** or **nail clippers**, but cutting wire will dull these tools.

Often pliers have a sharp edge that can be used for cutting wire. Use a **small file** for smoothing cut edges of wire or any rough spots.

Nylon-tipped hammer

• HAMMERS

A **nylon-tipped hammer** or **rubber-tipped hammer** is used to pound wire to strengthen it without changing the wire's round shape. A **household hammer** can be used to flatten wire. Be sure to work on a hard, protected surface, such as a stepping stone or brick.

• PROTECTIVE GEAR

Wire can be sharp at the ends and could cause injury if caution is not used. For safety, wear **goggles** when nipping wire and **protective gloves** such as cotton or leather gardening gloves when working with wire.

• JIGS & TEMPLATES

Jigs are templates for bending and winding wire. Commercially available jigs usually are made of plastic and have movable pegs of various sizes and shapes for creating a variety of patterns.

For some projects, instructions are given for creating templates or jigs from wood and dowels or nails for forming the wire. To make a template, you'll need:

Tracing paper for tracing the pattern for the template.
Transfer paper and a stylus for transferring the pattern.
Piece of wood for the template surface.
Small headless nails (3/4" wire brads work well in most cases) *or* **small diameter dowels** for forming the wire. If you make a template using dowels, you'll also need a drill with a drill bit to make the holes for the dowels.

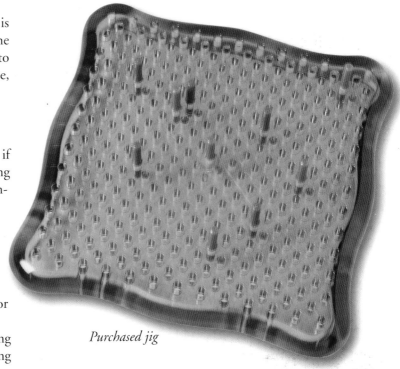

Purchased jig

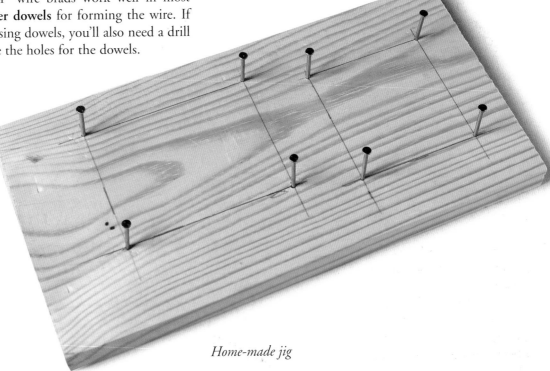

Home-made jig

Jewelry
&
Fashion
Projects

Black Faceted Heart Drop
necklace & earrings

Black bugle and seed beads and hematite squares are united around a faceted heart bead.
The matching earrings have French hook wires.

By Patty Cox

SUPPLIES

Black twisted bugle beads, 7mm

Black seed beads

Black E beads

Square hematite beads, 4mm

Black faceted heart bead with 4 side holes, 18mm

.012" beading wire

Silver spring ring clasp

4 silver crimp beads

Black beading thread and needle

2 gold French hook earring findings

TOOLS

Needlenose pliers

Wire cutters

INSTRUCTIONS FOR NECKLACE

The finished length is 18".

String the Necklace:

1. Cut two 22" lengths of beading wire.
2. Attach the clasp to one end of the two 22" lengths of wire with a crimp bead.
3. On both wires, thread:
   3 seed beads
   1 e bead
   3 seed beads
   1 twisted bugle bead
   Repeat this sequence six times.
4. On both wires, thread:
   3 seed beads
   1 e bead
   1 hematite bead
   1 e bead
   3 seed beads
   1 bugle bead
   3 seed beads
   1 e bead
   3 seed beads
   1 bugle bead
   3 seed beads
   1 e bead
   1 hematite bead
   1 e bead.
5. Separate the wires. On top wire, thread:
   3 seed beads
   1 bugle bead
   3 seed beads
   1 e bead
   3 seed beads
   1 bugle bead
   3 seed beads
6. On lower wire, thread:
   3 seed beads
   1 bugle bead
   3 seed beads
   1 e bead
   1 hematite bead
   1 e bead
   3 seed beads.
7. Thread wire through top hole of faceted heart.
8. Repeat beading sequence in opposite order for other side.
9. Attach other side of the clasp to the other end of the wire with a crimp bead.

Add the Dangle:

Black beading thread was used to make a flexible dangle.

1. Thread beading needle through lower holes of faceted heart. Add:
   11 seed beads
   1 e bead
   5 seed beads
   1 e bead
   1 hematite bead
   1 e bead
   2 seed beads.
2. Bring thread around last seed bead, then back through 10 beads.
3. Add 11 seed beads. Thread needle through faceted heart. Bring thread tails together at heart back. Tie off.

Instructions for earrings begin on page 20.

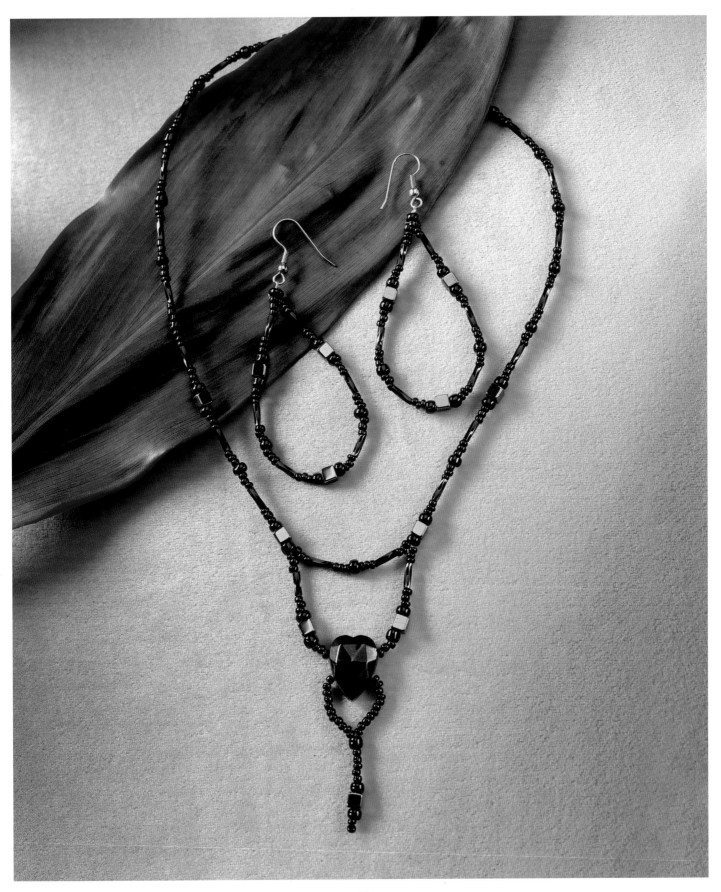

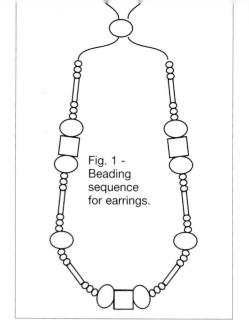

Fig. 1 - Beading sequence for earrings.

continued from page 18

Instructions for Earrings

See Fig. 1.

1. Cut a 7" length of beading wire. Thread beads on wire as shown in Fig. 1. Bring wire ends together.
2. Thread an e bead and a crimp bead on both wires. Fold wires over earring finding loop, then back through crimp bead. Pull taut. Secure crimp bead.
3. Run wire tails back through several beads. Trim excess wire tails.
4. Repeat steps 1 through 3 to make a second earring. ❏

Pearls & Wire Twists
choker

Using pink wire adds an element of surprise and a glow of color to a delicate necklace of white pearls.

By Patty Cox

SUPPLIES

26 gauge rose colored wire

2 silver crimp beads, size 2

Fuchsia-lined light blue seed beads

120 white pearls, 3mm

23 white pearls, 6mm

Silver spring ring clasp

TOOLS

Needlenose pliers

Wire cutters

INSTRUCTIONS

1. Cut three 1-yd. lengths of rose wire. Thread a crimp bead, then half of the spring ring clasp on all three wires. Fold wires over clasp ring. Slide crimp bead next to clasp over all wires. Crimp the bead.
2. Thread a 6mm pearl over all the wires. Cut wire tails.
3. Separate the three wires. Thread a 6mm pearl on the center wire. Thread eight seed beads on each outer wire. Pull all beads tightly toward clasp end. Twist wires 1/8".
4. On top outer wire, thread three 3mm pearls. Bring wire tightly back to the other two wires, forming the pearls into a triangle, then twist all three wires.
5. Repeat step 4 on the lower outer wire, then twist all wires 1/8".
6. Continue alternating 6mm pearls with seed beads and triangles of 3mm pearls to 15" or desired length.
7. End with a 6mm pearl, a crimp bead, and the other half of the clasp. Fold all wires over clasp ring and through crimp bead and pearl. Pull wires taut. Crimp the bead. Cut wire tails. ❏

Souvenir Coins
necklace & earrings

Use coins you've collected on vacation and millefiori beads to create this keepsake necklace and earrings.

By Patty Cox

SUPPLIES

8 millefiori beads, 8mm

Black E beads

15 souvenir coins

9mm black bugle beads

15 gold jump rings

.012" beading wire

Spring ring necklace clasp

2 crimp beads

2 gold French hook earring findings

2 gold eyepins

TOOLS

Needlenose pliers

Round nose pliers

Drill and 1/16" carbide drill bit

Vise grips

Wire cutters

INSTRUCTIONS FOR NECKLACE

The finished length is 21".

Drill:

1. Working one coin at a time, clamp the seven coins for the necklace in vise grips. Drill a 1/16" hole in the top of the coin.
2. Attach a jump ring in each coin hole.

Assemble:

1. Attach one side of the clasp to one end of a 25" length of beading wire with a crimp bead.
2. To string one side of the necklace, thread:

   4 repeats* (of e bead, 3 seed beads, bugle bead, 3 seed beads)

   1 e bead

   1 coin

   1 repeat*

   1 e bead

   1 millefiori bead

   1 repeat*

   1 e bead

   1 coin

   1 repeat*

   1 e bead

   1 millefiori bead

   1 repeat*

   1 e bead

   1 coin

   1 repeat*

   1 e bead

   1 millefiori bead

   1 repeat*

   1 e bead

   1 coin (This coin is at the center of the necklace.)

   One repeat = 1 e bead, 3 seed beads, 1 bugle bead, 3 seed beads.
3. Repeat step 2 in reverse to string the other side of the necklace.
4. Attach the other piece of the clasp to the other end of the wire with a crimp bead.

INSTRUCTIONS FOR EARRINGS

1. Working one coin at a time, clamp each of the eight earring coins in the vise grips. Drill a 1/16" hole in the top of each coin.
2. Drill three 1/16" holes along the bottom edges of two coins.
3. Connect three coin dangles (the ones with one hole) to each of the top coins (the ones with three holes in the bottom).
4. Thread a millefiori bead on an eyepin. Trim wire tail to 3/8". Form a loop in the wire tail, using round-nose pliers. Connect one loop to one top coin with a jump ring.
5. Connect other loop of that millefiori eyepin to an earring finding with a jump ring.
6. Repeat steps 4 and 5 to complete other earring. ❏

Grandmother's Photos
necklace

Supplies from the scrapbooking aisle provide the inspiration for this colorful necklace adorned with tiny children's photos.

By Patty Cox

SUPPLIES

.015" beading wire

Silver magnetic clasp

2 silver crimp beads

57 white pearls, 2mm

6 foil-covered round beads, 13mm

10 foil-covered round beads, 6mm

13 clear mosaic tile sticker squares, 3/8"

12 clear mosaic tile sticker squares, 1"

13 turquoise square scrapbooking frames, 3/8"

4 turquoise square scrapbooking frames, 1"

4 pink square scrapbooking frames, 1"

4 purple square scrapbooking frames, 1"

12 small jump rings

13 large jump rings

Photos of grandchildren

Computer, printer, and white paper *or* black fine-tip marker and white paper

Optional: Double-sided adhesive sheets, 13 additional clear mosaic tile sticker squares

TOOLS

Needlenose pliers

T-pin *or* large needle

Small metal punch *or* small nail and hammer

Wire cutters

INSTRUCTIONS

The necklace is 24" long.

Make the Letter Frames:

1. Photocopy the letters GRAND-CHILDREN *or* type and print them on your home computer.
2. Adhere a 3/8" mosaic tile sticker diagonally on each letter. Cut out along sticker edges.
3. Place each letter in a 3/8" turquoise frame. Press prongs flat in back. Repeat for all letters.
4. To add jump rings to letter frames, pierce a hole in the top corner of each letter tile with a t-pin or large needle. Insert large jump ring though hole.

Make the Photo Frames:

1. Adhere a 1" mosaic sticker diagonally on each photo. Cut out along sticker edges.
2. Place each photo in a 1" frame. Press prongs flat in back. Repeat for all 12 photos.

Option: Cover the back prongs with another photo and clear tile sticker, using double-sided adhesive on photo backs.

3. To add jump rings to photo frames, punch a small hole in the top corner of each photo frame, using a metal punch or a small nail and hammer. Insert a small jump ring through each hole.

Assemble:

1. Cut a 28" length of beading wire. Attach one half of the magnetic clasp to one end of wire with a crimp bead.
2. Thread beads, letter frames, and photo frames (on jump rings), using the photo as a guide.
3. Finish the necklace with the other half of the magnetic clasp and a crimp bead. ❑

Pattern for Letter Tiles

G R A N D

C H I L D R E N

Beads & Charms
necklace

Three inspirational words - "Live," "Love," "Laugh" - are stamped in polymer clay and highlighted with color and combined with wire-wrapped beads to make a charm-ing necklace.

By Patty Cox

SUPPLIES

24 gauge gold wire

7 bead charms

30 or more assorted green glass beads

Translucent polymer clay

Alphabet rubber stamps

Green dye *or* paint

Gold spring ring clasp, 6mm

Gold jump rings

Rubber stamps with words (Choose ones that make a deep impression.)

Wax paper

Spray gloss finish

TOOLS

Needlenose pliers

Roundnose pliers

Rolling pin

Wire cutters

INSTRUCTIONS

The necklace shown is 24" long.

Make Clay Charms:
1. Soften clay. Roll to 1/4" thickness between sheets of wax paper.
2. Press three of the bead charms into clay. Cover with wax paper. Roll over clay and charms with rolling pin. Remove clay-filled charms.
3. Cut three 3" pieces of gold wire. Insert a piece of wire through the side holes of each clay-filled charm.
4. Press a rubber stamp in each clay charm, making a deep impression.
5. Bake charm-filled clay. Let cool.
6. Rub paint or dye into crevices left by stamping in clay. Let dry.
7. Spray charms with gloss finish.

Make Wrapped Beads:
See Figs. 1, 2, and 3. The instructions are for one bead. Repeat for succeeding beads.
1. Cut a 6" length of gold wire. Hold wire 1" from end with roundnose pliers. Fold wire over round nose, forming a loop. Add a bead over both wires. (Fig. 1)
2. Form a loop on other end of wire next to bead, using roundnose pliers. Hold loop with pliers and wrap wire tightly around loop. (Fig. 2)
3. Continue spiraling wire around bead and end wire tightly around loop on other end of bead. Cut wire tails. (Fig. 3)
4. With needlenose pliers, grasp one wire wrap on bead. Twist needlenose to tighten wire and form a decorative bend in wire wrap.

Add Eyepins to Unwrapped Beads:
1. Thread each bead on an eyepin. Form a loop at the end of the eyepin.
2. Repeat for remaining beads.

Add Beads to Charms:
1. Pull out the wire from the charms.
2. Insert an eyepin into the side hole of one bead charm. Thread a bead on eyepin, then thread eyepin end through other side hole of bead charm. Form a loop at the end of the eyepin.
3. Repeat for remaining charms.

Assemble:
1. Connect all beads and charms with jump rings, using the photo as a guide.
2. Attach clasp at ends of necklace. ❑

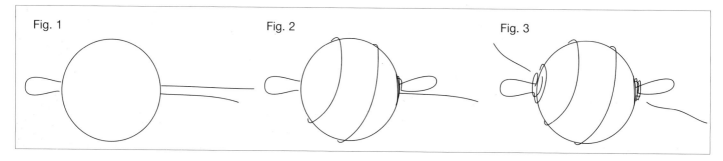

Fig. 1   Fig. 2   Fig. 3

Beaded Palms
bottle cap earrings

The blue palm-tree motif bottle caps make great casual earrings when framed
with blue seed beads.

By Patty Cox

SUPPLIES

4 bottle caps with an interesting
  design

.012" beading wire

6 crimp beads

Seed beads

French hook earring findings

Strong multi-purpose adhesive

TOOLS

Needlenose pliers

Metal punch

2 spring clothespins

Toothpick

Wire cutters

INSTRUCTIONS

Punch & Add Bead Trim:

1. Using a metal punch (photo 1) and working from the inside out, punch a hole in each dimple around the edges of two bottle caps. (photo 2)
2. Cut an 18" length of beading wire. Starting from the inside of bottle cap, thread wire through a hole leaving a 1" tail on the inside. Thread a crimp bead on tail. Crimp bead on the inside of bottle cap.
3. Thread five seed beads on wire. Thread wire through next hole to inside of bottle cap. Add one seed bead on the inside of bottle cap. (Fig 1) Loop wire around seed bead, then back through bottle cap hole. (Fig. 2) Thread wire back through the fifth seed bead on outer edge of bottle cap.
4. Thread four seed beads on wire. Thread wire through next hole to inside of bottle cap. Add one seed bead on the inside of bottle cap, loop wire around seed bead, then back through hole. (Fig. 3)

5. Continue adding beaded scallops around bottle cap. On the last scallop, add three seed beads to complete a five bead scallop. Bring wire to inside of bottle cap. Thread a crimp bead on wire. Pull taut. Crimp bead. (Fig. 4) Reserve wire tail for hanging loop.
6. Repeat on one other bottle cap.

Make Hanging Loops:

1. Thread wire tails on two beaded bottle caps from inside of bottle cap through one bottle cap hole, then back through another bottle cap hole. Add a crimp bead and crimp wire on inside of bottle cap. (Fig. 5)
2. Attach a French hook ear wire on each loop.

Assemble:

1. Apply glue on seed beads around inside of each bottle cap, using a toothpick.
2. Align bottle cap back, spokes, and dimples onto the back of the beaded bottle cap. Hold caps together with a spring clothespin. Allow glue to dry. ❏

Photo 4, attaching clasp

Photo 5

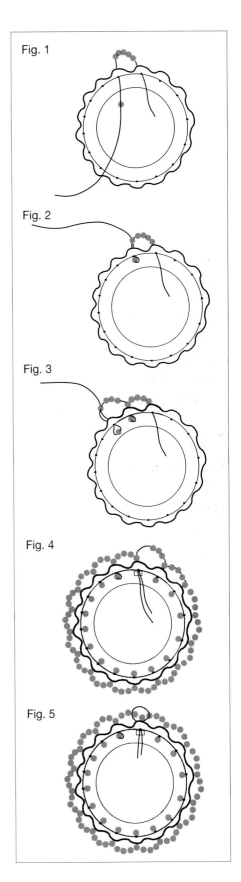

Fig. 1

Fig. 2

Fig. 3

Fig. 4

Fig. 5

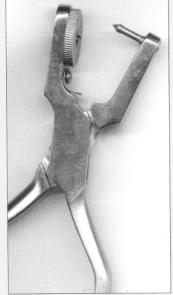

Photo 1 - The metal punch.

Photo 2 - The punched cap.

SUPPLIES

.012" beading wire

Turquoise round beads, 6mm

Frosted amethyst E beads, size 6

Frosted red E beads, size 6

Olive bicone faceted beads, 6mm

Magenta round glass beads, 6mm

Amber tubular beads, 20mm

Amber seed beads

Gold seed beads

Gold spring ring clasp

6 gold crimp beads

24 gauge gold wire

1-1/2" gold eyepins, 35

2 gold 3-hole connectors

Gold jump rings, 3mm

TOOLS

Needlenose pliers

Roundnose pliers

Nylon-jaw pliers

Wire cutters

Fig. 1 - Eyepin assembly with one loop and beads

Fig. 2 - Eyepin assembly complete

Fiesta
tri-strand necklace

This colorful necklace with a South-of-the-Border sensibility would make a simple outfit ready for a party. See the following pages for the matching bracelet and earrings.

By Patty Cox

INSTRUCTIONS

Load Eyepins:
Load 35 eyepins with 3/4" of assorted beads. First form a loop on the end of the eyepin, then add beads. (Fig. 1) Make a loop on the other end with roundnose pliers. Finished length should be 7/8" from loop to loop. (Fig. 2)

Make Wire Zig-Zags:
1. Make eight wire zig-zags by holding the eye of an eyepin with roundnose pliers. Use the tip of a needlenose pliers to bend the stem of the eyepin back and forth into a zig-zag.
2. Form a loop at the opposite end with roundnose pliers.
3. Flatten zig-zag with nylon-jaw pliers.

Assemble the Strands:
1. Center strand - Attach 13 beaded eyepins end to end with jump rings.
2. Middle strand - Attach 14 beaded eyepins end to end with jump rings.
3. Outer strand - Attach 16 beaded eyepins end to end with jump rings.
4. Attach the ends of each strand to a 3-hole connector with jump rings.

Assemble the Ends:
1. Cut two 14" lengths of beading wire.

Slide one half of the spring ring clasp to the center of one 14" length of stringing wire. Thread a crimp bead on wires next to clasp. Crimp the bead.
2. Holding both wires together, thread:
1 gold seed bead
1 frosted red e bead
1 gold seed bead
17 amber seed beads
1 gold seed bead
3 frosted amethyst e beads
1 gold seed bead
17 amber seed beads
1 gold seed bead
1 magenta 6mm bead
1 gold seed bead
17 amber seed beads
1 gold seed bead
1 olive 6mm faceted bead
1 gold seed bead
(This will be about 4-1/4" of beads.)
3. Separate the wires. Thread each wire with 17 amber seed beads and a crimp bead. Fold each wire over outer holes of 3- hole connector, then back through crimp bead. Tighten wire and crimp the bead. Thread wire tails back through several amber seed beads. Cut wire tails.
4. Repeat for other side of necklace, using the other half of the clasp. ❑

Fiesta
bracelet & earrings

Intended as companion pieces for the Fiesta Tri-strand Necklace, these colorful pieces can stand alone or be worn together.

By Patty Cox

SUPPLIES

.012" beading wire
Turquoise round beads, 6mm
Frosted amethyst E beads, size 6
Frosted red E beads, size 6
Olive bicone faceted beads, 6mm
Magenta round glass beads, 6mm
Amber tubular beads, 20mm
Amber seed beads
Gold seed beads
Gold spring ring clasp
6 gold crimp beads
24 gauge gold wire
1-1/2" gold eyepins, 37
French hook earring findings
6 headpins, 1-1/2"

TOOLS

Needlenose pliers
Roundnose pliers
Nylon-jaw pliers
Wire cutters

INSTRUCTIONS FOR BRACELET

Load Eyepins:
Load 35 eyepins with 3/4" of assorted beads by forming a loop on the end of the eyepin, then adding beads. (Fig. 1) Make a loop on the other end with roundnose pliers. Finished length should be 7/8" from loop to loop. (Fig. 2)

Make Wrapped Beads:
1. Cut a 9" length of gold wire. Hold wire 1" from end with roundnose pliers. Fold wire over round nose of pliers, forming a loop. (Fig. 3)
2. Add three 6mm magenta round beads over both wires. (Fig. 4)
3. Form a loop on other end of wire with round nose of pliers. Holding loop with round nose, wrap wire tightly around loop and continue spiraling wire around beads. (Fig. 5) End wire tightly around loop. Cut wire tails. (Fig. 6)

Make Wire Zig-Zags:
1. Make three wire zig-zags by holding the eye of an eyepin with roundnose pliers. Use the tip of a needlenose pliers to bend the stem of the eyepin back and forth into a zig-zag.
2. Form a loop at the opposite end with roundnose pliers.
3. Flatten zig-zag with nylon-jaw pliers.

Assemble:
1. Slide one half of the spring ring clasp to the center of a 20" length of beading wire. Thread a crimp bead on wires next to clasp. Crimp bead.
2. Separate wires. Add 17 amber seed beads and one gold seed bead on each wire.
3. Slide the looped ends of a beaded eyepin on each wire. Add a gold seed bead, three amber seed beads, and a gold seed bead on each wire.
4. Slide the looped ends of a beaded eyepin on each wire. Continue this sequence until bracelet is desired length.
5. Add 17 amber seed beads on each wire. Bring wires together.
6. Add a gold crimp bead and the other half of the clasp on double wires. Fold wires over clasp end, then back through crimp bead. Pull wires taut and crimp bead. Thread wire tails back through several amber beads. Cut wire tails. ❏

INSTRUCTIONS FOR EARRINGS
1. Thread one 20mm tubular bead on an eyepin. Form a loop on other end.
2. Load three headpins with 3/4" of assorted beads. Form a loop on the end of each headpin.
3. Attach the headpin loops to tubular bead loop with a jump ring.
4. Attach ear wire to top loop of earring.
5. Repeat to make other earring. ❏

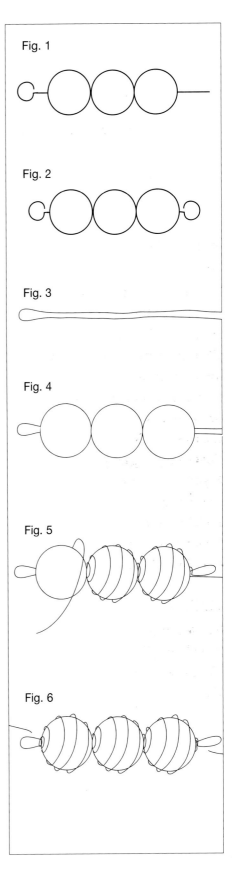

Fig. 1

Fig. 2

Fig. 3

Fig. 4

Fig. 5

Fig. 6

Art Glass Ensemble
necklace & earrings

Art glass beads provide color and dimension to this ensemble. They're combined with lighter, smoother glass beads that are easier on the ears and the back of the neck.

By Patty Cox

SUPPLIES

.015" beading wire

Glass lampwork eye beads, 9.5mm

9 glass lampwork multi round beads, 14mm

Czech glass beads, 8mm

Round silver washers, 6mm

Multi-colored glass E beads

2 fluted silver beads, 4mm

4 silver crimp beads

1 spring ring clasp, 6mm

2 silver French hook earring findings

TOOLS

Needlenose pliers

Wire cutters

INSTRUCTIONS FOR NECKLACE

This necklace is 24" long.

1. Cut a 26" length of beading wire. Thread a crimp bead and clasp on one wire end. Fold wire end over clasp, then back through crimp bead. Pull taut. Crimp the bead.
2. Thread a 4mm fluted silver bead next to clasp. Thread 2-3/4" of e beads, placing a seed bead between each e bead.
3. Thread beads in this sequence:
   washer
   8mm round
   washer
   seed bead
   e bead
   seed bead
   washer
   9.5mm eye bead
   washer
   seed bead
   e bead
   seed bead
   washer
   Repeat four times.
4. Thread beads in this sequence:
   14mm art glass multi-round
   washer
   seed bead
   e bead
   seed bead
   washer
   8mm round
   washer
   seed bead
   e bead
   seed bead
   washer
   Repeat three times.
5. Add a 14mm glass multi-round for the necklace center bead.
6. Repeat sequence in reverse for the other side of the necklace.

INSTRUCTIONS FOR EARRINGS

1. Cut a 7" length of bead stringing wire.
2. Thread five e beads, putting a seed bead between each e bead.
3. Add a:
   washer
   9.5mm eye bead
   washer
   seed bead
   e bead
   seed bead
   washer
   14mm glass multi-round bead.
   Repeat sequence in reverse for other side of loop.
4. Bring wire ends together. Thread a washer, a crimp bead, and a French hook ear wire loop on wires. Fold wires over ear wire loop, then back through crimp bead. Pull taut. Crimp the bead. Thread wire tails back through several beads. Cut excess wire tails.
5. Repeat to make the other earring. ❏

Turquoise Twists & Tassel
necklace

A mix of beads are unified by a single color and silver accents. The wire filigree twists are easy to make - you simply wrap wire on a craft stick, make loops, and gently twist with your fingers. The tassel is beaded on thread.

By Patty Cox

SUPPLIES

.012" beading wire

Silver crimp beads

Silver spring ring clasp

26 gauge peacock blue colored wire

6 cane turquoise blue glass beads, 13mm

9 cane turquoise blue glass beads, 8mm

1 blue matte donut bead, 10mm

6mm silver round washer spacers

Turquoise cat's eye beads - 8mm round, 6mm round, 4mm round, 10mm oval

Blue matte glass mix - Seed beads, bugle beads, E beads

Turquoise/purple flat AB mix - 8mm squares, diamonds, tubes

2 yds. beading thread and needle (for fringe)

Optional: Turquoise dye

TOOLS

Roundnose pliers

Needlenose pliers

Mini craft stick

Wire cutters

INSTRUCTIONS

Make the Blue Wire Twists:

1. Mark two lines on a mini craft stick 3/4" apart. (Fig. 1)
2. Place a 4" tail of blue wire along the edge of the craft stick. Wrap wire over tail and around craft stick. Compress wraps tightly to fit as many wraps as possible between the marks without overlapping the wire. (Fig. 1) Remove wire from craft stick.
3. Form a loop in first wire tail, next to wraps, using a roundnose pliers. Wrap second tail tightly around loop. Cut second tail. Thread first tail back through wraps. (Fig. 3)
4. Form a loop in tail wire next to wraps. Wrap tail tightly around loop. Cut excess tail wire. (Fig. 4)
5. Gently twist wire into a spiral with your fingers. (Fig. 5)
6. Repeat to make four spiral beads.

Continued on page 38

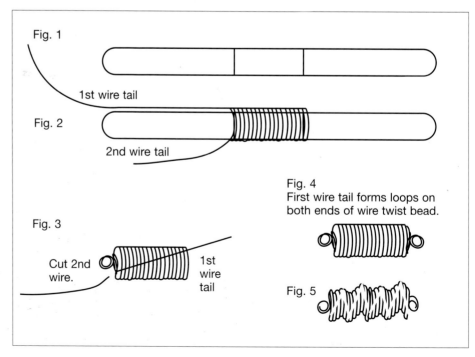

Fig. 1

1st wire tail

Fig. 2

2nd wire tail

Fig. 3

Cut 2nd wire.

1st wire tail

Fig. 4
First wire tail forms loops on both ends of wire twist bead.

Fig. 5

continued from page 36

Make the Tassel:

1. Using the beading thread and needle, wrap thread around donut bead three times and knot. Thread 3" of beads on thread. Bring thread around last bead of fringe, then back through all beads to donut. Wrap thread around donut and knot. (Fig. 6)
2. Repeat nine times to make the fringe of the tassel. Thread tails back through several beads of fringe.
3. *Option:* Dot turquoise dye on white threads around donut bead.

String the Necklace:

1. Cut a 9" length of beading wire. Attach half of the clasp to wire end with a crimp bead.
2. Thread 2-1/2" of beads on wire. Thread crimp bead and one loop of spiral twist bead on wire. Fold wire over loop, then back through crimp bead. Pull taut. Crimp the bead. Cut the tail.
3. Cut a 9" length of bead stringing wire. Attach spiral twist bead loop to wire end with crimp bead.
4. Thread 3-1/4" beads on wire. Thread a crimp bead and one loop of a second spiral twist bead on the wire. Fold wire over loop, then back through crimp bead. Pull taut. Crimp the bead. Cut the tail.
5. Cut an 18" length of beading wire. Attach spiral twist bead loop to wire end with a crimp bead.
6. Thread 4-1/2" beads on wire. This includes the 1-1/2" center drop. Bring thread around the donut tassel, then back through 1-1/2" of beads.
7. Thread 3" of beads on wire, then repeat steps in reverse to make the other side, ending with the other half of the clasp. ❏

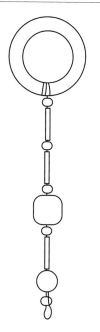

Fig. 6 - Donut bead with first strand of tassel.

Fig. 7 - The completed tassel on the center drop.

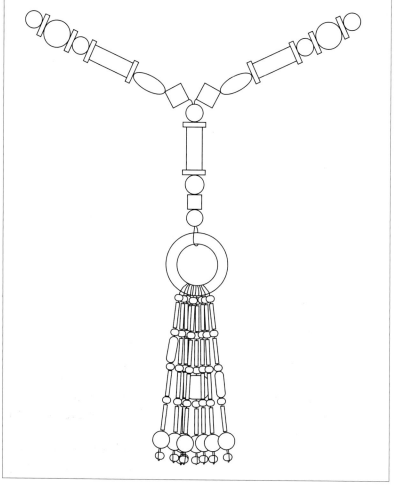

SUPPLIES

26 gauge silver wire

2 silver crimp beads, size 2

4 mint green cat's eye round beads, 6mm

6 oval pearls, 3mm x 6mm

5 crystal bicone faceted beads, 4mm

Crystal rainbow seed beads

Silver spring ring clasp

TOOLS

Needlenose pliers

Jig

Nylon-jaw pliers

Wire cutters

INSTRUCTIONS

1. Cut three 18" lengths of wire. Thread a crimp bead, then one side of the spring ring clasp on all three wires. Fold wires over clasp ring. Slide crimp bead next to clasp over all wires. Crimp bead.
2. Thread a 4mm cat's eye bead over all wires. Cut the short wire tails.
3. Separate the three wires. Thread an oval pearl on the center wire. Thread eight seed beads on each outer wire.

Fig. 1 - How to set pegs of jig

Green Cat's Eye
wire-twist bracelet

Gleaming cat's eye beads and pearls are framed with tiny crystal seed beads and alternated with filigree-framed crystal bicones.

By Patty Cox

Pull all beads tightly toward clasp end. Twist wires 1/4".
4. Place pegs in jig according to Fig. 1. Loop each outer wire around pegs. Remove from jig. Flatten wire loops with nylon-jaw pliers. *Option:*Pinch with fingertips.
5. Bring center wire back to center. Thread with a crystal bicone.
6. Following the wire filigree with bicone, twist all three wires together 1/4".
7. Separate the three wires. Thread a cat's eye on the center wire. Thread eight seed beads on each outer wire. Pull all beads tightly. Twist wires 1/4".
8. Continue adding pearls, filigree, and cat's eye beads to make a bracelet 9" long.
9. Attach other half of clasp at end of wires. Try on bracelet and adjust as needed. Slide a crimp bead over all wires and crimp to secure. Trim ends. ❏

Victorian Loops
necklace & earrings

A necklace of interlocking loops and coordinated earrings take their inspiration from the beaded jewelry of the Victorian era.

By Patty Cox

SUPPLIES FOR NECKLACE

.012" beading wire

Silver spring clasp

2 silver crimp beads

Mint rainbow seed beads

Clear glass faceted beads, 4mm

Olive luster glass faceted beads, 4mm

Olive luster glass faceted beads, 6mm

3 silver headpins

TOOLS

Needlenose pliers

Roundnose pliers

Wire cutters

INSTRUCTIONS FOR NECKLACE

1. Cut two 1-yd. lengths and one 1-1/2-yd. length of beading wire.
2. Attach half of the clasp to one end of the three lengths of beading wire with a crimp bead. (Fig. 1) Thread a 4mm faceted bead over the wire ends.
3. Thread 11 mint seed beads on one wire strand. Hold the remaining two wires together and thread 11 mint seed beads on the double wire strand. Thread one 4mm clear faceted bead on the double wire strand. Thread the other wire through the clear bead in the opposite direction. Pull wires together

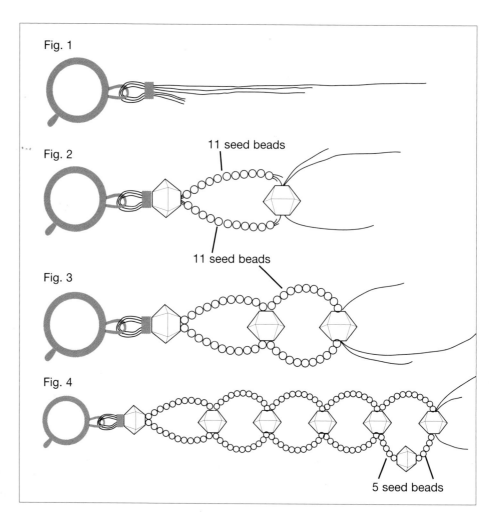

Fig. 1

Fig. 2 — 11 seed beads

11 seed beads

Fig. 3

Fig. 4

5 seed beads

forming a single weave. (Fig. 2) Continue, making another loop. (Fig. 3)

4. Continue working with the double wire strand for the next four single weaves. Add a small faceted olive bead on the fourth single weave with five seed beads on either side. (Fig. 4)
5. Bring the longest wire to the top. (This is your looping wire.) Make two more single weaves with short wires. (Fig. 5)

Continued on page 42

41

continued from page 40

6. Thread the looping wire with 28 seed beads. Loop wire down through a clear faceted bead. Add 9 seed beads, a 4mm olive faceted, a 6mm olive faceted, a 4mm olive faceted, and 9 seed beads. Run looping wire up through clear faceted bead. (Fig. 6)

7. Continue forming loops according to Figs. 7 and 8.

8. Create a bead dangle on the third loop. On a headpin, thread a seed bead, a 4mm olive faceted, a 6mm olive faceted, a 4mm olive faceted, and a seed bead. Form a loop on the end of the headpin, using round-nose pliers. Thread the looped end of headpin on the looping wire. (Fig. 9)

9. Continue working to necklace center, making the middle single weave larger, with 17 seed beads on the top and 9 seed beads on each side of the faceted beads on the bottom. (Fig. 11)

10. With the looping wire, form the large center loop with a dangle. (Fig. 11) From the center point, repeat following Fig. 11 in the opposite order to the end. Put the looping wire back into the single weave when all loops have been completed.

11. Attach the other half of the clasp to end of the three lengths of stringing wire with a crimp bead. Run wires back through 11 beads. Cut wire ends. ❏

SUPPLIES FOR EARRINGS

.012" bead stringing wire

2 silver crimp beads

Mint rainbow seed beads

Clear glass faceted beads, 4mm

Olive luster glass faceted beads, 4mm

Olive luster glass faceted beads, 6mm

2 silver headpins

2 silver French hook ear wires

INSTRUCTIONS FOR EARRINGS

Make Two Dangles:

1. Thread a 4mm olive, a 6mm olive, and a 4mm olive bead on each headpin. Trim wire end to 3/8".

2. Form a loop on headpin end.

Make Bead Loops:

Cut two 6" lengths of bead stringing wire. On each, thread 11 seed beads, a 4mm olive, a 6mm olive, one dangle, a 6mm olive, a 4mm olive, and 11 seed beads on wire. Bring wire ends together.

Complete:

1. Thread a 4mm clear faceted bead and a crimp bead on both wires of one earring. Fold wires over ear wire loop, then back through crimp bead. Crimp the bead.

2. Thread each wire back through several beads. Cut excess wire tails.

3. Repeat for second earring. ❏

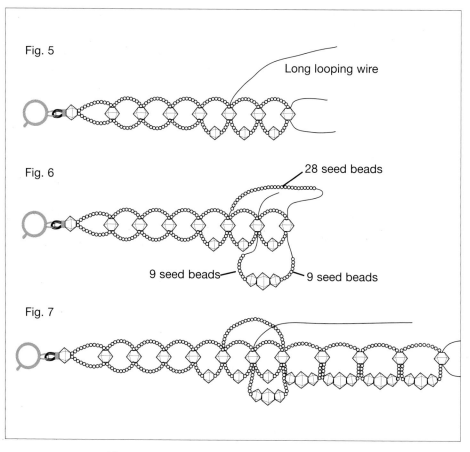

Fig. 5

Long looping wire

Fig. 6

28 seed beads

9 seed beads — — 9 seed beads

Fig. 7

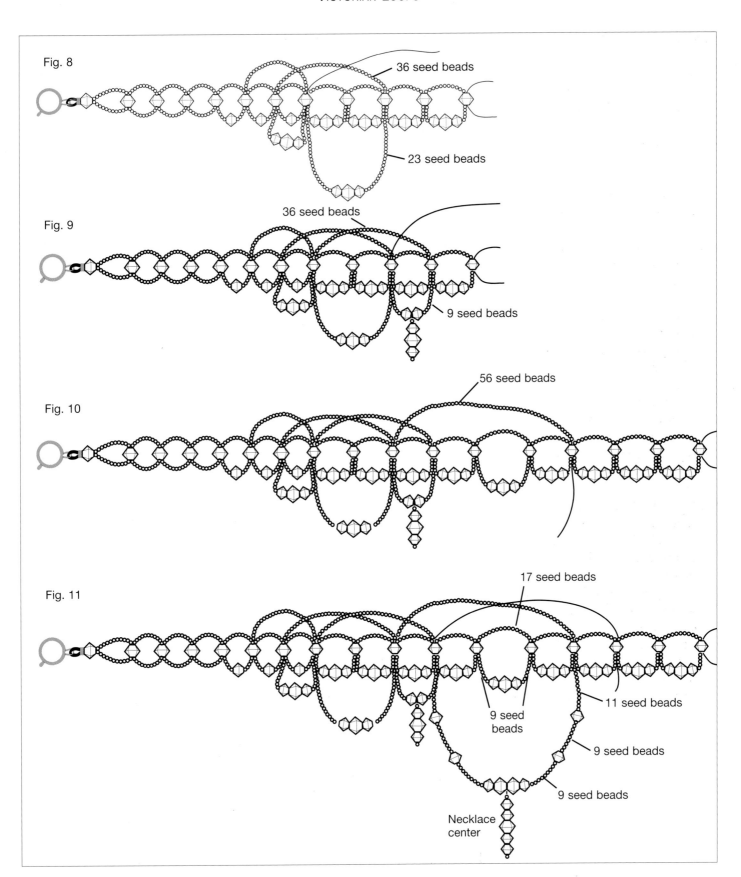

Fig. 8

36 seed beads

23 seed beads

Fig. 9

36 seed beads

9 seed beads

Fig. 10

56 seed beads

Fig. 11

17 seed beads

11 seed beads

9 seed beads

9 seed beads

9 seed beads

Necklace center

Asian Pendant
necklace

A dramatic red-and-black necklace is accented with three Asian coin pendants.

By Patty Cox

SUPPLIES

.015" beading wire

Gold crimp beads

1 Asian coin with center hole, 38mm

2 pre-drilled Asian coin pendants, 22mm

4 red art glass beads, 9mm

7 matte black bicone beads, 14mm

11 black E beads

16 red round beads, 6mm

5 red oval beads, 9mm

Black seed beads

8" gold chain

Gold barrel clasp

5 gold spacer bars, 10mm

24 gauge gold wire

Gold jump rings

TOOLS

Roundnose pliers

Needlenose pliers

Wire cutters

INSTRUCTIONS

Make Wrapped Beads:

1. Cut a 9" length of gold wire. Hold wire 1" from end with roundnose pliers. Fold wire over the round nose, forming a loop. (Fig. 1)
2. Add a 6mm red round bead, 9mm red oval and 6mm red round over both wires. (Fig. 2)
3. Form a loop on the other end of the wire with roundnose pliers. Hold loop with the round nose and wrap wire tightly around loop. (Fig. 3) Continue spiraling wire around beads. End wire tightly around loop. Cut wire tails. (Fig. 4)
4. Repeat steps 1 through 3 to make five wrapped beads.

Make Section 1:

See Fig. 5.

1. Cut a 7" piece of beading wire. Thread a crimp bead and half the barrel clasp on the wire end. Fold wire over barrel clasp, then back through crimp bead. Crimp the bead.
2. Thread on wire:
   2" seed beads
   a 6mm round
   1 e bead
   1 bicone bead
   1 e bead
   1 crimp bead
   1 wrapped bead

Continued on page 46

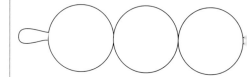

Fig. 1 - Wrapped beads, step 1.

Fig. 2 - Wrapped bead, step 2.

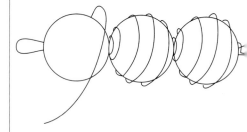

Fig. 3 - Wrapped beads, step 3.

Fig. 4 - Wrapped beads, step 4.

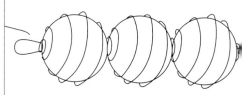

45

continued from page 44

3. Fold wire over loop of wrapped bead then back through crimp bead. Pull taut. Crimp bead.
4. Attach section 1 to top hole in coin (labeled "connector") with a jump ring.
5. Repeat to make the other side.

Make Section 2:
See Fig. 5.
1. Attach a wrapped bead to outer hole on coin (the connector) with jump ring.
2. Cut a 15" piece beading wire. Thread a crimp bead and a wrapped bead loop on wire. Fold wire over loop of wrapped bead then back through crimp bead. Crimp the bead.
3. Thread on wire:
   1 e bead
   1 bicone bead
   1 e bead
   a 10mm spacer
   a 6mm round
   1 seed bead
   a 9mm art glass bead
   1 seed bead
   a 6mm round
   a 10mm spacer
   1 e bead
   1 bicone bead
   1 e bead
   a 9mm art glass bead
   1 seed bead
   a 10mm spacer
   1 seed bead
   1 wrapped bead loop
   1 crimp bead
4. Wrap the wire end over the loop of the wrapped bead, then back through the crimp bead. Pull taut. Crimp bead.

5. Thread wire end back through a seed bead, a 10mm spacer, a seed bead, a 9mm art glass bead, and an e bead.
6. Repeat steps 1 through 5 in reverse for other side of necklace.

Make the Drop:
See Fig. 5.
1. Cut a 4" length of beading wire. Thread 1-1/2" of seed beads on the wire, ending with a crimp bead.
2. Thread the beaded wire through the bottom loop of a wrapped bead and through the center hole in the coin pendant. Thread wire end through crimp bead. Pull wire taut. Crimp the bead. Thread wire tails back through several seed beads. Cut excess wire tails.

Attach the Chain:
See Fig. 5.
Attach one end of the 8" chain to the center hole in one connector coin with a jump ring. Repeat on other connector coin.

Make & Attach the Center Strand:
See Fig. 5.
1. Cut an 11" length of beading wire. Thread a crimp bead on the wire. Fold wire end over inner hole of connector coin, then back through crimp bead. Crimp the bead.
2. Thread 3" of seed beads, a 9mm art glass bead, 3" of seed beads, and a crimp bead on the wire.
3. Fold wire end over inner hole of other connector coin, then back through seed bead. Pull taut. Crimp the bead. Thread wire tail back through several seed beads. Cut excess wire tail. ❏

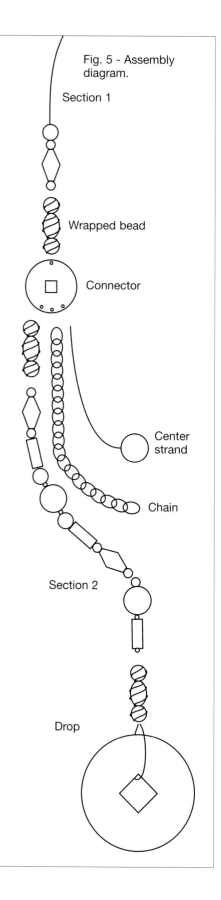

Fig. 5 - Assembly diagram.

Section 1

Wrapped bead

Connector

Center strand

Chain

Section 2

Drop

Jazzy Jeans
belt loop dangle

Jazz up your jeans or your purse with this beaded dangle. The basic design can be made with just about any beads in the color(s) of your choice. The split key ring holds it securely.

By Barbara Mansfield

SUPPLIES

22 gauge gold wire

5 beads, 15mm

6 gold metal beads, 10mm

1 bead, 6mm

3 long narrow beads

18 metal spacer beads, 5mm

Split key ring

TOOLS

Roundnose pliers

Wire cutters

INSTRUCTIONS

1. Cut three 5" pieces of wire. Make loop in the end of each piece.
2. For the two outside dangles, thread:
   a gold bead
   a 15mm bead
   another gold bead
   another 15 mm bead
   a long narrow bead
   5 metal spacers
   Make small loop on the end of each wire and clip wires.
3. For the center dangle, thread:
   the 6mm bead
   a gold bead
   a metal spacer
   a 15mm bead
   another gold bead
   a spacer
   a long narrow bead
   five spacers
   Make a small loop on the end and clip excess wire.
4. Thread the three dangles on the key ring. ❏

Pink Roses
choker

Rose-shaped beads are the focal point for this simple pink choker.

By Patty Cox

SUPPLIES

.018" beading wire

Silver spring ring clasp

2 silver crimp beads

Pink rainbow seed beads

Green-lined rocaille E beads

5 rose flower beads

TOOLS

Needlenose pliers

Wire cutters

INSTRUCTIONS

This necklace is 14" long.

1. Cut two 22" lengths of .018 beading wire. Attach half the clasp to one end of the two lengths with a crimp bead. (Fig. 1)

2. Thread one green rocaille on both wires. Thread 3/4" of pink beads on each wire strand. Thread one green rocaille on one wire. Thread other wire through rocaille. (Fig. 2) Pull wires together, forming a single weave loop.

3. Continue adding 3/4" of pink seed beads on each wire and threading wires through a rocaille bead to form a loop. Make six loops.

4. Make five more loops, substituting a rose bead to form the loop instead of the rocaille bead.

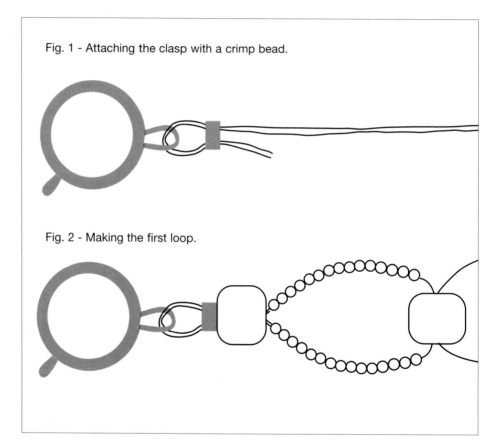

Fig. 1 - Attaching the clasp with a crimp bead.

Fig. 2 - Making the first loop.

5. Make seven more loops, again with a rocaille bead forming the loop.

6. End by threading a crimp bead, then the other half of the clasp to wires. Loop wires back into the crimp bead. Crimp bead with needlenose pliers. Thread wire ends through several beads. Cut wire tails. ❏

Amethyst & Filigree
adjustable choker & earrings

The chain extension on the choker allows you to adjust the length to accommodate
a variety of necklines. The wire filigree pieces are wrapped on a jig.

By Patty Cox

SUPPLIES

1-1/2 yds. .012" beading wire
Amethyst glass seed beads, size 6
Frosted amethyst seed beads, size 6
Amethyst bicone faceted beads, 6mm
Gold seed beads
Gold spring ring clasp
3" gold chain
2 gold crimp beads
24 gauge gold wire
14 gold headpins, 1"
2 French hook earring findings

TOOLS

Needlenose pliers
Roundnose pliers
Nylon-jaw pliers
Wire cutters
Jig

INSTRUCTIONS FOR NECKLACE

Make the Wire Filigree Pieces:

1. Cut a 9" length of 24 gauge gold wire. Place pegs in jig according to Fig. 1.
2. Form a small loop in one wire end with roundnose pliers. Place loop on top peg of jig. Wrap wire around pegs according to diagram. Form wire loop at bottom peg. Remove wire from jig and cut wire tail.
3. Flatten wire with nylon-jaw pliers.
4. Thread an amethyst bicone bead on a headpin. Cut wire tail of headpin to 1/2".
5. Using roundnose pliers, form a loop in wire end. Attach loop to bottom loop of filigree piece.
6. Bend filigree top loop perpendicular to the flattened design.
7. Repeat steps 1 - 6 to make 10 more pieces (11 in all).

Assemble the Necklace:

1. Slide spring ring clasp to center of the 1-1/2 yd. length of stringing wire.

Thread a crimp bead on both wires next to clasp. Crimp the bead.
2. Thread an amethyst bead, a gold seed bead, and a frosted amethyst bead on the double wire strand. Continue adding beads in this sequence for 2".
3. Separate wires. Thread one gold seed bead on one wire strand. Thread other wire in opposite direction through seed bead. (Fig. 2) Pull wires taut.
4. On the top wire, thread a frosted amethyst bead, a gold seed bead, a frosted amethyst bead, and a gold seed bead. (Fig. 3)
5. On the bottom wire, thread an amethyst bead, a gold seed bead, a frosted amethyst bead, a gold seed bead, a filigree piece, an amethyst bead, a gold seed bead, and a frosted amethyst bead. (Fig. 3)
6. Thread the bottom wire through gold seed bead on top wire. (Fig. 3) Pull wires taut.
7. Bring the two wires back together. Thread an amethyst bead on both wires. (Fig. 4) Separate wires. Thread one gold seed bead on one wire strand. Thread other wire in opposite direction through seed bead. (Fig. 4) Pull wires taut.
8. Continue, forming 11 weaves with filigree pieces and following steps 4 through 6.
9. Bring wires back together. Thread an amethyst bead, a gold seed bead, and a frosted amethyst bead on the double wire. Continue adding beads in this sequence for 2".
10. Slide a crimp bead, then the end link of the gold chain on the two wires. Fold wires over chain link, then back through crimp bead. Pull wires and crimp the bead. Thread wire tails back through several amethyst beads. Cut wire tails.
11. Thread a frosted amethyst bead on a headpin. Cut wire tail to 1/2". Using roundnose pliers, form a loop in wire end. Attach bead dangle at end of chain.

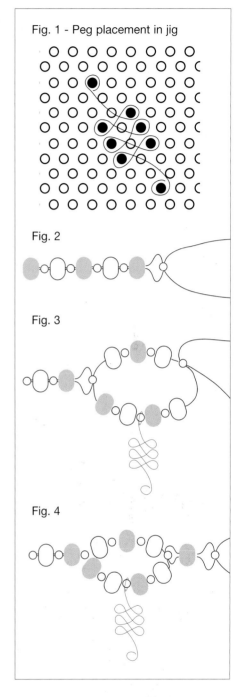

Fig. 1 - Peg placement in jig

Fig. 2

Fig. 3

Fig. 4

INSTRUCTIONS FOR EARRINGS

1. Make two filigree pieces on the jig, following the instructions in the "Make the Wire Filigree Pieces" section above.
2. Attach top filigree loop of each piece to an ear wire. ❏

Beads & Clay Charms
headband

A simple wire headband, adorned with shimmering polymer clay beads,

becomes jewelry for your hair.

By Ann Mitchell, AnKara Designs

SUPPLIES

Pearl polymer clay (You'll use 1/4 of a 2 oz. block.)

2 oz. bottle translucent liquid polymer clay

Grape glitter

Aluminum metal leaf

2 small leather or rubber stamps

Cornstarch

Wire headband with teeth

28 gauge purple wire

13 purple AB beads, 6mm

12 headpins

TOOLS

Toaster or convection oven

Oven thermometer

Flat baking tray

Oven mitts

Metal palette

Wooden craft stick

Paper towels

Wire cutters

Needlenose pliers

Polymer clay blade

Measuring spoons

INSTRUCTIONS

Make the Polymer Clay Beads:

1. Condition the polymer clay. Roll out a 1/4" snake of clay.
2. Place the clay snake over the sheet of aluminum leaf at one edge. Gently roll the snake to cover it in leaf. Trim the leaf when the snake is completely covered. Roll the clay snake gently to adhere the leaf to the clay.
3. Use the clay blade to cut the clay snake into 1/4" slices. (You need 12 slices for the headband.).
4. Dust the small stamps with cornstarch. Turn one stamp textured side up. Lay one slice of clay on the upturned stamp, then press down on the clay slice with the other stamp, textured side down. Gently press the clay between the stamps.
5. Slide a headpin through the bead while it is between the stamps. Release the bead.
6. Repeat steps 4 and 5 to stamp all the clay slices, re-dusting the stamps as necessary.
7. Bake the beads on the headpins for 20 minutes at 275 degrees F. Allow to cool.
8. Mix 1 teaspoon liquid polymer clay with 1/2 teaspoon of grape glitter to make a glaze. Using your finger, apply glaze to one side of each bead, allowing the glaze to settle into the textured surface of the bead. Wipe off excess with a paper towel.
9. Bake for 10 minutes at 275 degrees F. Allow to cool.
10. Glaze the other side of each bead and bake for an additional 10 minutes. Allow to cool.

Assemble:

1. Cut 2 ft. of purple wire. Holding the headband with the teeth down and starting at the end closest to you, wrap the wire around the headband base five times to secure it.
2. Thread one 6 mm bead on the wire. Pull the bead down flush with the headband. Wrap the wire around the next tooth on the headband. Thread a clay bead on the wire, pull the bead flush with the headband. Because the clay bead is larger, skip one tooth and wrap the wire around the next tooth. Continue alternating glass beads and clay beads around the entire headband. Wrap the wire five times around the headband to secure it after the last bead.
3. Clip off the excess wire and use needlenose pliers to pinch down the loose end. ❏

SUPPLIES

Gold polymer clay
  (You'll need 1/4 of a 2 oz. block.)
2 oz. bottle translucent liquid polymer clay
22 gauge magenta colored wire
24 gauge burgundy colored wire
Seed beads - Mixed metallics, burgundy
  striped
Fire-polished faceted garnet glass beads,
  4mm
Fire-polished faceted garnet glass football-
  shaped bead, 8mm x 12mm
Mica pigment powder - Super bronze
Polymer clay varnish

TOOLS

Brayer *or* pasta machine (dedicated to clay)
Work surface (granite, marble, acrylic, or
  ceramic tile)
Toaster oven
Oven thermometer
Oven mitts
Flat baking tray
Craft knife
Jig with pegs
Roundnose pliers
Nylon-jaw pliers
Wire cutters
1/2" flat brush (for varnish)
Brush cleaner
Small pointed brush (for mica powder)
Ruler
Paper towels
Wax paper

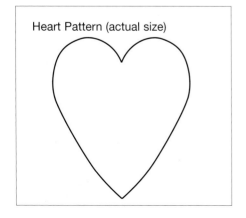

Heart Pattern (actual size)

Braided Beads with Filigree Heart
necklace

This heart pendant, made from polymer clay and decorated with wire filigree and mica powder, hangs from three braided bead strands.

By Karen Mitchell, Ankara Designs

INSTRUCTIONS

Make the Looped Trim:

1. On the jig peg board, place pegs in all the holes along one of the straight edges.
2. Cut a 16" piece of the magenta 22 gauge wire. Wrap the wire from one end of the jig to the other, forming a loop around each peg. When you reach the last peg, lift the wire off of the pegs, and place the last loop over the first peg. Continue, looping the wire around each peg to the end of the peg board. Once again place the last loop over the first peg, and repeat the looping a third time. Remove the wire from the pegs.
3. Use the nylon-jaw pliers to flatten and set the wire loops.
4. Place the wire loop trim over the heart pattern and carefully shape the trim into a heart shape with the round-nose pliers. The loops should face outward and follow the outside edge of the pattern. Handle and manipulate the wire carefully, so as not to damage the colored finish. Clip off the excess wire after forming the heart shape.

Make the Clay Heart:

1. Condition the gold polymer clay by kneading and rolling several times or by running through the pasta machine several times. Roll the clay into a sheet 1/8" thick. Place sheet on a small piece of wax paper on top of your work surface.
2. Spread a thin coat of liquid polymer clay over the surface of the gold clay sheet. Press the heart-shaped wire edging into the surface of the gold clay sheet. Trim away excess clay around the edge of the wire trim with a craft knife. Smooth the edges of the heart.
3. Cut a 3-1/4" piece of the 24 gauge burgundy wire. Form a 1/16" loop at one end. String burgundy striped seed beads on the wire, leaving 1/4" at the end of the wire. Form another 1/16" loop at the other end.
4. Form a small scroll at each end of the wire, with scrolls rolling towards each other. Hold one scroll over the left side of the heart just inside the wire trim. Measure to the bottom of the heart, and bend the wire into a "V" at the inner point of the heart, so that the second scroll is at the bottom right hand side off the heart. Press the beaded wire into the clay.
5. Cut 1-1/4" and 1-1/2" pieces of burgundy wire. Form a 1/16" loop at one end of each piece. String mixed metallic seed beads on each piece of wire leaving 1/4" at each end. Form 1/16" loops at the ends.
6. Form each wire into a single scroll. Place the larger scroll at the upper right side of the heart and the second scroll in the center. Press the scrolls into the surface of the clay.
7. Roll three 1/8" balls of gold clay. Place each ball on the clay heart between the beaded scrolls. Dab a light coat of liquid clay on the surface of each ball. Press a

Continued on page 56

continued from page 54

4mm faceted glass bead into the center of each ball, sinking the beads halfway into the clay.

8. Cut a 1-1/4" piece of magenta wire. Bend it in the middle with the round-nose pliers forming a 1/4" loop. Twist the ends together, and trim twisted ends to 1/4". Cut a 1-1/4" piece of magenta wire and form a 1/8" loop using the same method.

9. Dip the twisted end of the larger loop in liquid clay and insert it into the top of the heart perpendicular to the surface of the heart. Dip the twisted end of the smaller loop in liquid clay and insert it into the bottom tip of the heart with the loop parallel to the surface of the heart.

10. First with a small pointed brush and then your fingertip, coat the front and back surfaces of the clay heart with super bronze mica powder. Wipe the excess powder off the surface of the beaded scrolls with a paper towel.

11. Place the heart on the baking tray and bake for 20 minutes at 275 degrees F. Allow the heart to cool.

12. Varnish the front of the pendant. Allow to dry.

13. Varnish the back. Allow to dry.

Make the Drop:

1. Cut a 2" piece of burgundy wire. Form a 1/16" loop at one end.

2. Slide on the faceted garnet glass football bead, a metallic seed bead, a 4 mm faceted garnet glass bead, and another seed bead.

3. Using roundnose pliers, form a 1/8" loop in the wire above the beads. Hook this through the bottom loop on the heart, close the loop, and twist the wire several times around the base of the loop. Trim off excess wire, and fold in the trimmed end.

Make the Strands:

1. Cut three 24" pieces of burgundy wire. Twist together the ends for 2-1/2". Form a 1/4" loop 1-3/4" from the end of the twisted section. Twist the ends of the wires around the base of the loop. Trim excess wire and flatten any sharp ends.

2. String 18" of metallic seed beads on one of the three wires. Bend the wire around the last bead to keep the beads from sliding off.

3. On the second strand of wire, string 18" of burgundy striped seed beads, bending the wire gently at the last bead.

4. On the third strand of wire, string 4mm garnet glass beads, bending the wire at the end.

Assemble:

1. Braid the three strands of beads together for 7-1/2". Slide the heart pendant over the strand of 4mm faceted beads to what will become the center of the necklace. Continue braiding the three strands for another 7-1/2".

2. Straighten the wire at the end of each strand of beads. Remove beads, if needed, so that all the strands are the same length. Twist all three strands of bare wire together for 3-1/2" and trim off the excess wire. Bend the twisted end over 1-1/2" from the end. Wrap the remaining wire around the bottom 1/4", up to the beaded section. Trim and bend in sharp ends. Press at the fold in the wire so there is no loop. Perpendicular to the bend in the end of the wire, form a hook 3/4" from the end of the beaded section. Make sure it fits through the loop on the other end of the necklace. ❑

Chandelier Loops
earrings

Copper-toned polymer clay beads, amber crystal beads, orange faceted glass beads, and sparkling rondelles are combined to make these dangling earrings. Wear them and be memorable!

By Ann Mitchell, AnKara Designs

SUPPLIES

Silvertone 20 gauge wire

Silver polymer clay (You'll need 1/8 of a 2 oz. block.)

2 oz. bottle translucent liquid polymer clay

Copper glitter

2 silvertone lever-back earring hooks

8 amber AB bi-cone crystal faceted beads, 4mm x 6mm

4 orange faceted glass beads, 4mm x 6mm

6 clear iridescent faceted crystal beads, 10mm

16 clear/silver crystal rondelles, 5mm

16 silvertone headpins, 1-1/2" to 2"

TOOLS

Jig

Roundnose pliers

Needlenose pliers

Wire cutters

Mallet (the kind used in leather crafting)

Pad

Toaster or convection oven

Oven thermometer

Flat baking tray

Oven mitts

Metal palette

Wooden craft stick

Paper towels

Polymer clay blade

Measuring spoons

INSTRUCTIONS

Make Clay Beads:

1. Condition the silver clay and roll it into a 3/8" thick snake. Cut one end off so it is flat. Cut off two 3/8" long slices. Roll each slice into a ball.
2. Roll the clay snake so it is 3/16" thick. Cut off one end so it is flat. Cut four 3/16" slices. Roll each slice into a ball.
3. Squeeze 1/2 teaspoon liquid polymer clay into a metal palette. Add 1/8 teaspoon copper glitter. Stir completely, using a craft stick, adding more glitter if necessary to create a good, coppery mix.
4. Dip the first ball of clay into the copper liquid clay and roll the ball between the palms of your hands to get a solid coat of glitter on the bead. Keep dipping and rolling the bead until there is an even coat of copper glitter on the surface of the ball.
5. Insert a headpin through the center of the ball to make a bead, sliding the headpin all the way into the ball so the head is flush with the side of the bead.
6. Repeat steps 4 and 5 for the five other balls of clay.
7. Bake all six beads on the headpins for 20 minutes at 275 degrees F. Allow beads to cool.

Form Wires:

1. Place one thin peg in the jig at the corner. Place another thin peg along the diagonal 5/16" from the first peg. Place the 3/16" peg along the diagonal 1-1/4" from the second peg. On either side of the larger peg, place three thin pegs in a curving diagonal pattern. The first peg on each side should be about 1/4" from the center peg, the other two on each side should be evenly spaced about 3/16" away from the first thin pegs. The pattern should be symmetrical. Cut two 10" pieces of silver wire.
2. Place the end of the wire running just beyond the first peg. Wrap the wire in a figure eight pattern, starting with the second peg. Pull the wire taut as you wrap the pegs. Bring the wire down to the first peg on one side of the bottom of the earring shape. Continue to follow the pegs, making loops around each one. Bring the wire back up to the top peg.
3. Remove the large peg and carefully lift the wire off the pegs. Wrap the longer end of the wire twice around the center of the figure eight. Clip the excess of both pieces of wire and tuck under sharp ends, using needlenose pliers.

4. Place the wire earring pieces flat on the pad with the figure eight hanging off the edge. Pound the lower half of the earring shapes a few times with the mallet to harden the wire. **Do not** pound the loop and twist at the top.
5. Repeat steps 2 through 4 to make the second earring shape.

Add Beads:

1. Open the loop on the lever-back earrings. Hook on the wire shape, and gently close.
2. Place a 10mm clear iridescent bead on each of six headpins. Add a rondelle, then an orange bead to each headpin. On two of those headpins, add an amber AB crystal bead.
3. On each of six headpins, place a clay bead. To each headpin, add a rondelle and an orange bead. On the two headpins with the larger clay beads, add an amber AB crystal bead.
4. On each of four headpins, place an orange bead, a rondelle, and then an amber AB crystal bead.
5. At the top of each beaded headpin, form a loop with roundnose pliers. Clip off the excess wire.

Assemble:

1. On one wire shape, hook the drop with the crystal iridescent, orange, and amber beads to the loop in the middle of the earring shape and close the loop.
2. Hook the drop with the large clay bead from the large loop at the bottom of the earring shape and close the loop.
3. Hook two drops with the clear iridescent and orange beads on either side of the center drop. Close the loops.
4. Hook two drops with small clay beads next to the crystal drops, and close the loops.
5. Hook two drops with orange beads to the outermost small loops. Close the loops.
6. Repeat steps 1 through 5 to make the second earring. ❑

SUPPLIES

Purple polymer clay (You'll need 1/2 of a 2 oz. block.)

2 oz. bottle translucent liquid polymer clay

Mica pigment powder - Violet

5/8" faceted purple glass stone with flat or pointed back

22 silver faceted glass beads, 6 mm

40 silver twisted bugle beads, 7 mm

16-1/2" memory wire

18" silvertone 18 gauge wire

2 silvertone 3/4" headpins

1 silvertone jump ring, 1/4" diameter

Polymer clay varnish

TOOLS

Ballpoint pen *or* texturing tool

Roundnose pliers

Nylon-nose pliers (for wire manipulation)

Heavy duty wire cutters

1/4" paint brush

Brush cleaner

Work surface (granite, marble, ceramic tile, or acrylic sheet)

Toaster or convection oven (preferably dedicated to clay)

Flat baking tray

Oven thermometer

Oven mitts

Pasta machine (dedicated to clay)

1" round cutter (dedicated to clay)

Patterns (actual size)

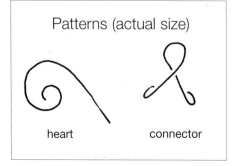

heart   connector

Filigree Pendant
choker

Memory wire makes an easy-to-wear choker that holds
a polymer clay and wire pendant.

By Karen Mitchell, Ankara Designs

INSTRUCTIONS

Bend the Wire Shapes:

1. Cut four 4" pieces of 18 gauge wire. Set aside the remaining 2". Bend each 4" piece in half with roundnose pliers. On the first piece, open the bend to about a 60-degree angle. Form a loop around the end of the roundnose pliers, leaving a 1/8" opening. Use the nylon-nose pliers to continue to form a spiral. Repeat for the other end of the wire. The two spirals should touch to form a heart shape. Flatten the heart completely with the nylon-nose pliers to set the wire shape.
2. Repeat to make four heart shapes.

Make the Clay Piece:

1. Condition the purple clay. Roll it through the pasta machine on the #1 setting. Cut out a 1" circle.
2. Spread a thin coat of liquid clay on the surface of the clay circle. Arrange the four wire hearts to form a clover shape with the points meeting in the center of the purple clay circle. Press the wire halfway into the clay.
3. Roll a 5/8" ball of purple clay. Flatten the ball to form a 3/16" thick disc. Center the disk over the purple clay circle and press it gently on the clay.
4. Spread a thin coat of liquid polymer clay on the surface of the disc. Center the glass stone over the disc and sink it into the disc.
5. Use the dull end of the craft knife to make decorative lines between each wire heart. Use a ballpoint pen or texturing tool to make decorative dots in between each line on the top edge of the disk.
6. With the tip of your finger, brush a light coat of violet mica powder on the textured clay around the stone.
7. Bake the pendant for 20 minutes at 275 degrees F. Allow to cool.
8. Apply a coat of polymer clay varnish to the clay portion of the pendant. Allow to dry.

Make the Connector:

1. Bend the reserved 2" piece of 18 gauge wire in half and form a 3/16" loop. (The ends should spread about 1/2" apart.) On each end, make a 1/8" loop perpendicular to the center loop, but don't close either loop.
2. Hook both loops to one of the wire heart shapes, using the photo as a guide. Close the connecting loops.
3. Attach the 1/4" jump ring to the top loop of the connector. Close the jump ring.

Assemble:

1. Using roundnose pliers, make a closed loop at one end of the memory wire. Slide 2 bugle beads, then 1 faceted 6mm bead on the wire. Repeat this pattern nine more times.
2. Slide the jump ring with the pendant on the memory wire. (This is the center of the necklace.)
3. Slide one silver 6mm faceted bead and two bugle beads on the memory wire. Repeat this pattern nine more times.
4. Form a loop at the other end of the memory wire.
5. Place a silver 6mm faceted bead on a headpin and make a loop. Clip off the excess wire. Hook the drop on one end of the memory wire. Close the loop.
6. Repeat to make a second drop for the other end of the memory wire. ❏

Heart of Fashion
wooden box purse

Beads, jewels, and wire swirls adorn the side of a colorful
and fun wooden box purse.

By Kathi Bailey

SUPPLIES

18 gauge copper wire

Red bugle beads, #3

Rhinestones, 3mm

Red rocaille beads, 10/0

Assorted crystal costume jewelry

Wooden box purse with handle

80 grit sandpaper

Acrylic craft paints - Black, Warm
   White, Lipstick Red

White jewelry glue

Liquid clear matte sealer

TOOLS

Wire cutters

Pencil

Masking tape

Foam brush

INSTRUCTIONS

Paint:

1. Using the photo as a guide, draw a
   rectangular, rounded shape on the
   front of the box. (This is the inset.)
   Tape off the shape.
2. Paint inside tape with two coats
   Warm White. Let dry and sand
   between coats. Let last coat dry and
   remove tape.
3. Tape over white edges and paint
   remainder of box but not the handle
   with two coats Black. Let dry and
   sand between coats.
4. Paint handle with two to three coats
   Lipstick Red. Let dry and sand
   between coats.

Decorate:

1. Draw 2" heart on white inset area.
   Fill area with glue, then fill with red
   rocaille beads. Let dry.
2. Cut pieces of wire and bend to make
   swirls and/or other shapes. Glue to
   inset surface, using the photo as a
   guide for placement.
3. Attach other beads and jewelry,
   scattering them over the white
   rectangle inset.
4. Cut a piece of copper wire to fit
   around the inset shape. Bend to fit
   the shape of the inset. Glue in place.
   Glue a row of bugle beads, end to
   end, along the outside edge of the
   wire. Let dry.
5. Cut 36" copper wire and wrap
   around handle. Insert ends of wire
   under the wrapped wire edges.
6. Glue more bugle beads on the
   handle holder. Let dry.
7. Seal with clear matte sealer, using a
   foam brush. ❏

Basic Black & Pearls
cigar box purse

A black-and-gold cigar box is dressed up and ready to go with a pearl and black bead handle. It's a fun way to give a new look to old costume jewelry.

By Kathi Bailey

SUPPLIES

27 pearls, 8mm

8 black faceted crystal beads, 8mm

1 large silver bead

2 black crystal beads, 5mm

Flat gold metal beads

Assorted pearl and crystal costume jewelry

Cigar box with labels intact

White jewelry glue

Gold metallic elastic cord

Black thick cord

24 gauge gold wire

TOOLS

Drill and drill bit

Wire cutters

INSTRUCTIONS

Make Closure:

1. Drill two holes in purse top, spacing the holes the width of the large silver bead with two small black beads on either side.
2. Place the black cord through the beads and pull the ends of the cord through the drilled holes to inside of purse. Knot the cord inside purse, trim the excess cord, and put glue on the knot for extra strength.

3. Drill two holes in purse front, near top, spaced around 1/2" apart. To make the closure loop, cut elastic to length, allowing extra for knotting, twisting, and trimming. Put ends of elastic in drilled holes. Close purse to check the length of the elastic by positioning it around the closure beads on the top. When you have the correct length, knot the elastic cord inside purse. Put glue on the knot for extra strength.

Make Handle:

1. Drill two holes on top of purse approximately 8" apart.
2. Cut 18" gold wire for handle. String on the wire 3 pearls, 1 black bead, 3 pearls, 1 black bead. Repeat the sequence until you reach the end of the wire, leaving enough wire to insert and secure in the holes. Knot wire inside purse, trim excess, and put glue on the knots for extra strength.

Decorate:

1. Cover drilled openings and the elastic with a large piece of jewelry and glue in place.
2. Scatter other beads and jewelry over the front of the purse and glue to adhere. ❑

Stylin'
beaded leather pouch

This pouch is as stylish as it is practical — and easier than you think. A beautiful beaded strand is used for a handle of a simply-made leather pouch. The pattern for this design is versatile as well. The pouch shown is designed to carry only the barest of necessities such as money, credit cards and cell phone. As seen on the front and bottom of this pouch, many remnant ends have natural cut edges that can be wrapped or overlapped for use as an interesting accent. Upholstery leather can be found at your nearest leather store or on-line.

By Lisa Galvin

SUPPLIES

Upholstery leather piece with at least one natural cut edge (size shown here in Red leather measures approx. 6-1/4" x 10")

3/16" post back line 20 snap in antique bronze

Contact cement

Black awl thread

Super Sheen Leather finish spray

8 Black plated crimp beads, size #1 (1.3mm)

49 strand beading wire

Ruby and jet black cut glass rectangle beads

8mm faceted beads

Black E beads

Metalized bronze and gold seed beads

2 Black 1/8" eyelets with liner

Black rubberstamp pigment ink pad

TOOLS

Leather shears

Scratch awl

Ruler

Wire cutters

Bead crimping pliers

Eyelet Setter

Snap setter

1/8" round hole drive punch

Mallet

Punch board

Hairdryer

INSTRUCTIONS

Making Pouch:

1. Cut a leather piece 6-1/4" x 10" (or the size of your choice). Leave one "rough cut" end for an authentic western look on the finished pouch. Fold piece in thirds, width wise; overlapping rough cut edge at front. Apply contact cement to overlap portion only and press together with palm of hands.

2. Cut bottom edge of pouch as desired or adapt using natural cut edges as is shown here. Trim excess as needed. Apply a 1/2" band of cement to inside bottom edge of purse and press together to adhere.

3. To create decorative stitching at top of pouch, use scratch awl and corner of punchboard to punch a row of small holes that are 1/4" apart and 1/4" from top edge of pouch. This will allow needle to easily pass through the leather when hand stitching. Thread embroidery needle with a 40" length of black awl thread. Knot thread end. Beginning at one side edge; blanket stitch around top to put a finishing touch on pouch opening. Once back at starting point whip stitch 3 - 4 times and slide threaded needle through stitching on inside of pouch to secure end. Trim excess thread.

4. SNAP CLOSURE: Place pouch onto punchboard and use 1/8" round hole drive punch and mallet to punch a hole approximately 3/4" from top edge, going through both leather layers so that snap will align properly when finished. Insert tube shaped snap end through hole at front of pouch, slide on snap back piece and set using snap setting tool. Repeat to attach remaining snap and opposite inner snap piece to back of pouch.

5. EYELETS FOR NECK STRAP: Measure 1/2" from top edge then mark and punch a 1/8" hole at each side edge of pouch. Insert eyelet through hole on outside of pouch, position liner on back side and use eyelet setter and mallet to set. Repeat for opposite side.

6. Give pouch an authentic "antique" effect by lightly pressing Black rubber-stamp ink pad around all outer edges; rubbing slightly to smooth. (TIP: Because inkpads may vary; for best results try on a scrap piece of leather to determine desired effect.) Heat lightly with blow dryer set on warm setting to set ink and prevent smudging. Spray with Super Sheen leather sealer to finish and protect surface. Set aside to dry.

Bead Accent:

Dangling bead accents may be added to one or more bottom edges of pouch by punching a small hole through leather with scratch awl to attach. Use needle to slip desired beads onto remaining length of awl thread. Insert needle through hole in front side of pouch, bring around bottom edge then back through pouch front again. Pull taunt. Slip additional beads onto thread and knot end to secure. Trim thread ends.

Beaded Strap:

See Fig. 1.

1. Cut a piece of beading wire that is approximately 8" longer than you wish handle length to be.
2. Slide two black crimp beads onto one end of beading wire, allowing about a 1/2" tail of wire. Do not crimp beads yet.
3. Add a ruby glass bead rectangle, an E bead, and two more black crimp beads.
4. String E beads and seed beads onto wire to create a 3/4" length from last crimp bead.
5. Slide end of wire through eyelet hole, from outside of pouch to inside.
6. String additional E beads and seed beads onto wire to create a 3/4" length.
7. Take end of wire up through crimp beads, ruby rectangle bead and the first two crimp beads. Adjust wire
8. Use crimping pliers to flatten crimp beads, securing wire end.
9. String beads onto wire in a pleasing

pattern, using the photo as a guide. Add beads until you have the desired length for the strap. For best results concentrate the larger glass beads near top of pouch; scattering a few throughout the strap for continuity.

10. Attach remaining wire end to pouch just as with first side. ❏

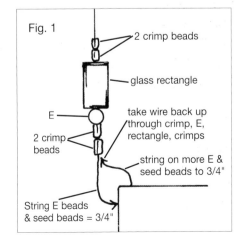

Fig. 1

2 crimp beads

glass rectangle

E

2 crimp beads

take wire back up through crimp, E, rectangle, crimps

string on more E & seed beads to 3/4"

String E beads & seed beads = 3/4"

Dreamy
box purse

This purse is a dream to make and to use. A small wooden box is decorated with rubber stamps and enhanced with a beautiful beaded handle. So simple yet so beautiful.

By Lisa Galvin

SUPPLIES

Wooden trunk style box purse (size shown here: 7-1/2" x 5-5/8" x 3-3/4")

Acrylic craft paint, Raw Sienna

Decoupage medium, matte finish

Rubber stamps: Swirls, Butterfly, and Word "dream"

Embossing ink pad

Gold embossing powder

Double-sided super sticky tape, 1/4" wide

Gold tiny glass marbles

Six 16mm x 10mm antique gold Tunisian old world beads

Brown lampwork glass beads: one 24mm x 12mm barrel bead and two 15mm x 10mm round

Acrylic crystal faceted beads: two 12mm bicones, two 15mm faceted

Two 12mm x 5mm round clear acrylic disc beads

12" length 12 gauge wire, any color

Multi-purpose adhesive

Black felt for lining (optional)

Double-sided tape sheet to attach lining (optional)

TOOLS

Screwdriver

Sandpaper, fine grit

Tack cloth

1" flat brush

Heat gun

Scrap paper

Scissors

Ruler

Drill with appropriate size drill bit

Pliers

INSTRUCTIONS

Decorating Purse:

1. Remove any hinges or other hardware from box (if at all possible) using screwdriver. Lightly sand to remove any rough areas then wipe with tack cloth to remove dust.
2. Drill two holes in box lid that are large enough for wire to comfortably slip through.
3. Basecoat box with Raw Sienna acrylic craft paint, using 1" paintbrush. Apply two coats to entire box surface, inside and out. For best results allow paint to dry completely between coats.
4. Decorate one side of box at a time. Stamp box with swirls, butterflies, and words, using embossing ink and referring to photo for placement. With a scrap piece of paper used to catch excess, pour embossing powder over stamped images to coat. Return excess embossing powder back into container for use on remaining sides of box. Use heat gun to emboss, following manufacturers' directions. Repeat for all sides. NOTE: For best results, heat powders only briefly as prolonged heating in one area may bubble paint. (TIP: Scrap piece of paper can be used to "mask off" some areas of box, if needed, when stamping.)
5. Brush box, inside and out, with two or more coats of decoupage medium. For a more "texture-like" effect, brush in various directions when applying medium.
6. Cut two pieces of double-sided super sticky 1/4" tape that are 1/2" longer than front and back of box width. Peel backing and press into a bowl of gold mini marbles to coat one side of each tape strip. Peel backing away and attach to box lid, on front and back.

Beaded Handle:

1. Slide beads onto beading wire in the following order: clear acrylic disk, antique gold Tunisian bead, crystal acrylic bicone, round lampwork bead, faceted crystal acrylic bead, two Tunisian, barrel style beads, lampwork bead, two Tunisian barrel beads, crystal acrylic bicone, round lampwork bead, crystal bicone, Tunisian barrel bead, clear acrylic disk.
2. Insert your own beaded wire handle through holes in lid and bend at right angles on inside of box. Glue in place.

Finishing Purse:

1. To line purse, cut a piece of double-sided tape sheet to fit inside top and bottom of box and one 1/4" smaller than the outside bottom of purse. Apply tape to felt, cut felt to fit.
2. Apply the appropriate pieces to bottom on both inside and outside of box and to top inside of box lid.
3. Reassemble purse; attaching all hardware that was previously removed. ❑

Projects
for
the
Home

Beaded Place Setting
napkin ring & placemat trim

Beads and wire look great on your table. Make each set in different colors for a personalized effect, or make identical multiples for a coordinated look.

By Patty Cox

SUPPLIES

.012" beading wire

24 gauge burgundy colored wire

Metallic gold seed beads

Transparent gold seed beads

Purple bicone faceted beads, 4mm

Tortoise round beads, 4mm

Olive oval faceted beads, 8mm

Red round beads, 4mm

Gold bicone faceted beads, 4mm

Frosted purple round beads, 4mm

Round amber beads, 6mm

Square amber beads, 10mm

2 gold crimp beads

24 gauge gold wire

Gold eyepins

Placemat

TOOLS

Needlenose pliers

Roundnose pliers

Nylon-jaw pliers

Jig with pegs

Beading needle and thread

Wire cutters

INSTRUCTIONS FOR NAPKIN RING

1. Load eyepins with 7/8" of assorted beads. (Fig. 1) Form a loop on end of eyepin. (Fig. 2) The finished length of the beaded eyepin should be 1" from loop to loop.
2. Cut about 7" of 24 gauge burgundy wire. Form a small loop in one wire end with roundnose pliers. Place loop on top peg of jig. Wrap wire around pegs according to Fig. 3. Form wire loop at bottom peg. Remove wire from jig. Cut wire tail.
3. Flatten wire with nylon-jaw pliers. Bend filigree top loop perpendicular to the flattened design. Make three filigree pieces for each napkin ring.
4. Cut two 12" pieces of beading wire. String each wire with the looped end of a beaded eyepin. Add a gold seed bead, a faceted bugle bead, and another gold seed bead on each wire. Slide the looped ends of a beaded eyepin on each wire. Continue this sequence until the napkin ring is 6-1/2".
5. Add a gold crimp bead on each wire. Thread opposite ends of wires through crimp beads. Pull wires taut. Crimp beads. Thread wire tails back through several beads. Cut wire tails.

INSTRUCTIONS FOR PLACEMAT

Beads are sewn on placemat edges to make an evenly spaced fringe.

1. Using beading thread and needle, thread on a bugle bead, a gold seed bead, a 6mm bead, and a gold seed bead.
2. Bring thread around last seed bead on fringe, then back through all the beads. Knot thread on placemat edge. Cut thread. ❏

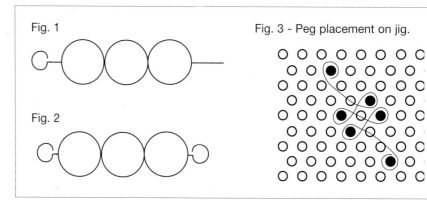

Fig. 1

Fig. 2

Fig. 3 - Peg placement on jig.

Pearly Grapes
wine bottle & glass charms

Think of them as a necklace for a bottle and bracelets for stemmed glasses. Present them with a special bottle and a couple of glasses for a great anniversary gift.

By Patty Cox

Closeup of bottle charm

SUPPLIES

1-1/2 yds. 26 gauge rose wire
2 silver crimp beads, size #2
White pearls, 3mm
16 pearls, 6mm
4 silver jump rings, 6mm
16 silver headpins

TOOLS

Needlenose pliers
Roundnose pliers
Jig with pegs
Wire cutters

INSTRUCTIONS FOR BOTTLE CHARM

1. Cut three 18" lengths rose wire. Thread a crimp bead, then a jump ring on all three wires. Fold wires over ring. Slide crimp bead next to ring over all wires. Crimp the bead. Cut wire tails. Twist three strands of wire together 1/8".
2. Place pegs in jig according to Fig. 1.
3. To make the filigree, loop each outer wire around pegs as shown in Fig. 1. Remove wire from jig. Flatten wire loops with nylon-jaw pliers or simply pinch with your fingertips. Bring

Continued on page 74

continued from page 72

middle wire back to center. Thread with a pearl, and center the pearl in the shaped wire. Pinch the three wires back together, then twist wires 1/4".

4. Form 15 pearled filigrees with 1/4" wire twists between each.

5. Bring both twisted wire ends together through a crimp bead. Crimp the bead. Cut wire tails.

Make the Pearl Grape Cluster:
See Figs. 2 and 3.

1. Thread one pearl on a headpin. Cut wire 3/8" beyond pearl. Using roundnose pliers, form a loop in wire end. Make 16.

2. Thread three pearls with loops on a jump ring. Add a second jump ring and three more pearls with loops.

3. Thread three pearls, one jump ring (the third), and two pearls on second jump ring.

4. Thread two pearls and one jump ring (the fourth) on the third jump ring.

5. Thread pearl on fourth jump ring.

6. Attach cluster to bottle band with 26 gauge rose wire.

INSTRUCTIONS FOR GLASS CHARM

1. Cut three 10" pieces of rose wire. Thread a crimp bead, then one jump ring over all three wires. Fold wires over ring. Slide crimp bead next to ring over all wires. Crimp the bead. Cut wire tails. Twist three strands of wire together 1/8".

2. Following the instructions above, make five pearled filigrees with 1/4" wire twists between each. Bring twisted end wires together. Twist wires 1/2".

3. Thread a crimp bead on wires at twisted ends. Crimp the bead. Cut wire tails.

4. Fold over 1/2" of twisted wires to make a hook. Shape charm into a circle. Put the hook through the jump ring on the other end. ❏

Closeup of glass charm

Fig. 1 - Peg placement on jig.

Fig. 2 - Jump ring assembly (without most of the pearls)

Fig. 3 - Jump rings with pearls

1st ring - 6 pearls

2nd ring - 5 pearls

3rd ring - 4 pearls

4th ring - 1 pearl

Beads on a Wire

hanging vase

To make this vase, you can buy pre-wired seed beads or string your own. The instructions list supplies for stringing your own. Use it to hold a welcoming bouquet on the guest room door.

By Barbara Mansfield

SUPPLIES

4 yds. 24 gauge wire
Seed beads, various sizes -
  Amethyst, lime, clear
Household cement
Glass vase, 4" diameter

TOOLS

Roundnose pliers
Wire cutters

INSTRUCTIONS

1. String 4 yds. amethyst, lime, and clear seed beads on 24 gauge wire. *Option:* Use purchased pre-wired beads.
2. Wrap beads around neck of vase, leaving a 12" tail. Wrap three or four times, then wrap the beads around the vase at an angle, wrap around the bottom of the vase, and wrap back up to the neck of the vase at an angle on the opposite side of the vase.
3. Repeat step 2, crossing the beaded wires as you go from top to bottom and bottom to top. Save a 12" piece to join the beginning tail and twist two to three times to secure.
4. Twist the tails together and make a loop, twisting together at the end.
5. Use glass cement to glue and secure the wires as needed. ❑

Bells & Rings

ringing bell pull

Hang this where the brass bells will catch the breeze and delight you with their sound.

By Patty Cox

SUPPLIES

Springs from a gold plate hanger that holds a plate 8"-11"

.018" beading wire

Gold crimp beads

Gold spacer beads, 4mm

Round faceted glass beads, 8mm

Oval faceted glass beads, 8mm

Bicone faceted glass beads,6mm

Faceted glass tube beads, 13mm

5 brass bells, 20mm

4 gold rings, 2" diameter

1 gold ring, 3" diameter

TOOLS

Needlenose pliers

Wire cutters

INSTRUCTIONS

Top Ring:

1. Remove springs from plate hanger rods.
2. Cut an 8" piece of beading wire. Thread a crimp bead on the wire. Fold wire over one 2" ring, then back through crimp bead. Crimp the bead.

Section 1:

See Fig. 1.

Thread 1-1/2" of beads and gold spacers on wire, ending with a crimp bead. Fold wire over a second 2" ring,

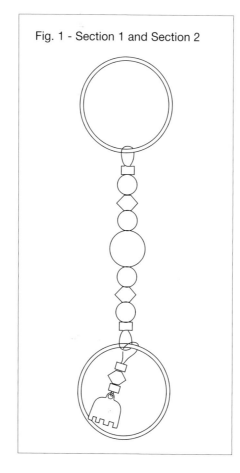

Fig. 1 - Section 1 and Section 2

then back through crimp bead. Crimp the bead. Run the wire tail back through the gold bead. Trim wire tail.

Section 2:

See Fig. 1.

Attach a 4" wire to a bell with a crimp bead. Add a bicone bead and another crimp bead. Fold wire over top of second ring through the loop of the connecting wire, then back through crimp bead. Crimp the bead. Run wire tail back through bead. Trim wire tail.

Section 3:

1. Cut an 8" length beading wire. Thread crimp bead on wire. Fold wire over lower part of second 2" ring, then back through crimp bead. Crimp the bead.
2. Thread 2-1/2" of beads and gold spacers on wire. Fold wire over spring end loop, then back through crimp bead. Crimp the bead. Run wire tail back through gold bead. Trim wire tail.
3. Thread 2-1/2" of beads and spacers below spring. Connect this beaded section to another 2" gold ring. Add a bell and bicone bead to ring,

Section 4:

1. Attach another beaded section with a spring below the third ring.
2. Attach a 3" ring to the end. Add a bell and two beads inside 3" ring.

Section 5:

Add a 2-1/2" beaded section below 3" ring. Attach a 2" ring to the end. Add a bell and a bicone bead to ring.

Section 6:

Attach a 5" beaded section with bell at the end to the lower part of last 2" ring. ❏

Photo Charms
magnetic frames

Display these fun fringed photo frames on your fridge.

By Patty Cox

SUPPLIES

Supplies are for one frame.

26 gauge colored wire

Seed beads

Plastic slide frames

2" square of flexible magnetic sheet

Double stick foam tape

Photograph to fit slide frame opening

Cellophane tape

TOOLS

Needlenose pliers

Craft knife

Wire cutters

INSTRUCTIONS

Make Bead Fringe:

1. Cut 2 yds. colored wire. Load wire with about 4" of seed beads.
2. Using needlenose pliers, form three 1/2" bends in wire spaced 1/8" apart. Slide a bead in each bend. (Fig. 1)
3. Hold the seed bead at the end of the bend and twist the wire. (Fig. 2)
4. Make three more bends in the wire. Continue forming beaded wire twists for 8".

Assemble:

1. Trim photograph as needed to fit the slide frame opening. Tape picture on frame back with cellophane tape.
2. Cut magnetic sheet just slightly smaller than the slide frame. Round corners.
3. Cover non-magnet side of magnetic sheet with double stick foam tape. Remove paper backing from foam tape.
4. Stick straight edge of wire twist fringe along edge of foam tape. Center and stick the front of the slide frame (with mounted photo) on foam tape so front of photo shows through opening in front of magnetic sheet frame.
5. Arrange wire twist fringe around frame. ❏

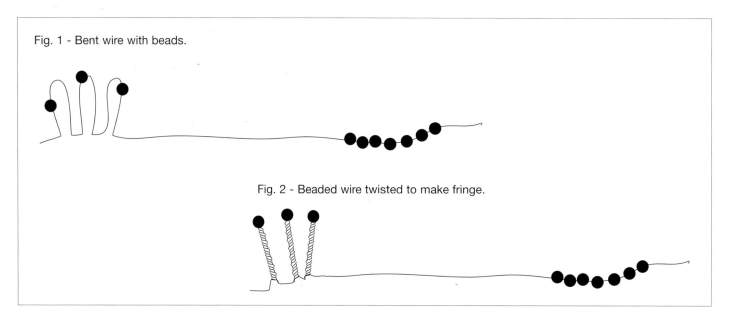

Fig. 1 - Bent wire with beads.

Fig. 2 - Beaded wire twisted to make fringe.

Candlelight Fringe
votive candle holder trim

Beads and wire add sparkle and shine to candle holders on the table.

By Patty Cox

SUPPLIES

Glass votive candle holder

.012" beading wire

24 gauge burgundy colored wire

Metallic gold seed beads

Transparent gold seed beads

Purple bicone faceted beads, 4mm

Tortoise round beads, 4mm

Oval olive faceted beads, 8mm

Round red beads, 4mm

Gold bicone beads, 4mm

Frosted purple round beads, 4mm

15 crystal faceted drops with loops

Gold crimp bead

Gold jump rings

24 gauge gold wire

Gold eyepins

Household cement

Candle

TOOLS

Needlenose pliers

Roundnose pliers

Nylon-jaw pliers

Jig with pegs

Wire cutters

INSTRUCTIONS

Make Filigree Pieces:

1. Cut 7" of 24 gauge burgundy wire.
2. Form a small loop in the end of one wire with roundnose pliers. Place loop on top peg of jig. Wrap wire around pegs according to Fig. 1. Form wire loop at bottom peg.
3. Remove wire from jig. Cut wire tail. Flatten wire with nylon-jaw pliers. Bend filigree top loop perpendicular to the flattened design.
4. Repeat to make 15 filigree pieces.

Make Wrapped Beads:

1. Cut 6" of gold wire. Hold wire 1" from end with roundnose pliers. Fold wire over the round nose, forming a loop. Add a 6mm red bead over both wires. (Fig. 2)
2. Form a loop on the other end of the wire with roundnose pliers. Hold the loop with the round nose and wrap wire tightly around loop. (Fig. 3)
3. Continue spiraling wire around bead. End wire tightly around first loop. Cut wire tails.

Continued on page 82

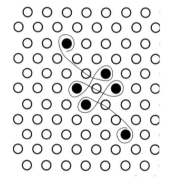

Fig. 1 - Peg placement on jig.

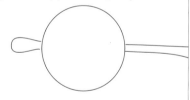

Fig. 2 - Wrapped bead, step 1.

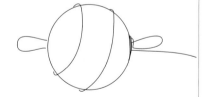

Fig. 3 - Wrapped bead, step 2.

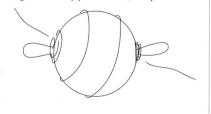

Fig. 4 - Wrapped bead, step 3.

continued from page 80

Assemble Beaded Dangles:
See Fig. 5.
1. Working from top to bottom, attach a wire filigree piece to an eyepin with:
   a gold seed bead
   a purple bicone bead
   a gold seed bead
   a tortoise round bead
   a gold seed bead
   an 8mm olive oval bead
   a gold seed bead.
2. Add a wrapped red bead, then an eyepin with:
   a gold seed bead
   a gold bicone bead
   a gold seed bead
   a tortoise round bead
   a gold seed bead
   a 4mm frosted purple bead
   a gold seed bead
3. Attach a faceted drop with a jump ring.
4. Repeat steps 1 through 4 to make 15 dangles.

Make the "Tiara":
1. Measure the circumference of the top of your votive. Divide that number by 16. The result equals the length of the space (the "determined space length") between each beaded dangle.
2. Cut two pieces of beading wire, each the length of the circumference + 4". Thread transparent gold seed beads on each wire to determined space length. Bring wires together. Thread a beaded dangle on the double wires.
3. Separate wires and add gold seed beads to determined space length. Continue alternating seed beads and dangles to circumference length.
4. Thread all wires through a crimp bead. Pull taut. Crimp the bead. Cut wire tails.

Install:
1. Place wires on top of votive. Separate wire scallops over rim of votive.
2. Dot areas with household cement to secure. Let dry. Add candle. ❏

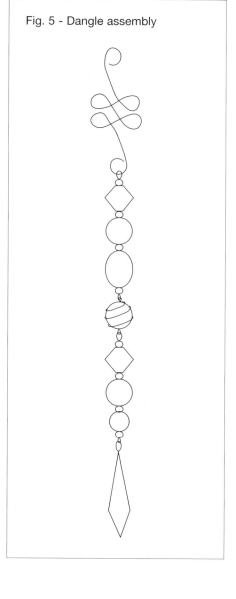

Fig. 5 - Dangle assembly

SUPPLIES

32 gauge gold wire

Green glass drawer pull, 1-1/4"

Light mint green seed beads

14 mint green round beads, 4mm

Frosted bead with large center hole, 18mm

Optional: Household cement

TOOLS

Wire cutters

INSTRUCTIONS

Make Fringe:

1. Cut 20" of gold wire. Thread 5" of seed beads on wire. Add a 4mm bead, then another 5" of seed beads. Bring wire ends together evenly, then twist together with the 4mm bead on the bottom. Twist top wires to secure beads. (This is one strand of fringe.)

2. Repeat to make 14 strands.

Assemble:

1. Holding all strands of fringe so they are even at the bottom, twist top wires together.

2. Thread twisted wires through drawer pull, then through the 18mm bead. Fold twisted wire over, forming a loop. Slide the 18mm bead up and twist the wire to secure the loop. Push bead down over the wires. Drip ceramic and glass cement in the top hole of the bead.

3. Cut another 20" piece of wire. Thread 10" of seed beads on wire. Fold wire in half with the beads evenly distributed. Twist bead strands together, leaving about 4" of wire untwisted. Wrap twisted beads around fringe top. Secure in place with wire ends. Cut wire tails.

4. *Option:* Dot wrap with glue. ❏

Tasteful Tassel
furniture tassel

Hang this beaded tassel as you would a silk tassel - attach it to a key on an armoire or use it to adorn a drawer pull. The large green "bead" is a vintage style glass drawer pull. The beaded fringe is strung on wire.

By Patty Cox

Retro Bottle Caps
clock

This retro wall clock evokes the moderne style. The wire-wrapped arms come out of the center like the spokes on a wheel. They are quick and easy to make with an electric drill.

By Patty Cox

SUPPLIES

5" wooden disc

3 wooden dowels, 1/8" diameter, 36" long

12 bottle caps

Spool of 24 gauge wire

White enamel spray paint

Red enamel paint

Quartz movement clock works

Strong multi-purpose adhesive

Gloss enamel spray finish

Optional: 12 red felt circles, 1" diameter

TOOLS

Protractor

Needlenose pliers

Drill with 1/8" and 1/4" drill bits

Pencil

Saw

Scouring pad

Piece of plastic foam

Wire cutters

INSTRUCTIONS

Prepare the Pieces:

1. Find center of wooden disc. Divide disc into 12 equal parts and mark on the back with a pencil.
2. Drill a 1/4" hole through the center of the disc. Drill a 1/8" hole in the side of the disc at the 12 places you marked.
3. Cut dowels into 9" lengths.
4. Insert a 9" dowel and the end of 24 gauge wire into drill. Secure ends in drill. (Fig. 1)
5. Switch drill to slow speed. While slowly running the drill, hold the wire next to the dowel and allow the wire to tightly coil around dowel. *Finger Saving Tip:* Use a scouring pad to hold the wire next to dowel; the scouring pad also prepares the wire for painting. Let the wire coil around the dowel to 1/2" from the end.

Paint:

1. Insert ends of coiled wrapped dowels

in plastic foam. Spray coil-wrapped dowels with white paint.
2. Spray paint hands of clock with white spray paint. Let dry.
3. Paint disc front and sides and 12 bottle caps with red enamel. Let dry.
4. Spray with gloss enamel finish. Let dry.

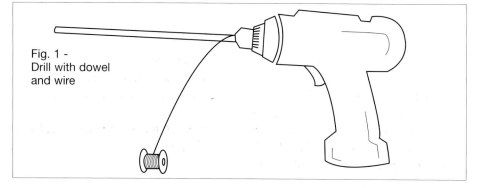

Fig. 1 -
Drill with dowel
and wire

Assemble:

1. Squeeze a small amount of adhesive in one of the holes on the side of the disc. Insert a coil-wrapped dowel. Repeat for all 12 spokes of clock.

2. Trim the 12 o'clock, 3 o'clock, 6 o'clock, and 9 o'clock dowels to 7-1/2". Cut away ends with wire cutters.

3. Trim all other dowels to 7".

4. Place clock disc face down on a flat surface. Fill bottle cap backs with adhesive. Place a glue-filled bottle cap under each spoke end. Allow glue to dry.

5. Insert clock movement on back of disk and through center hole. Attach clock hands to center post.

6. *Option:* Glue red felt circles on backs of bottle caps. ❏

Dragonfly Sushi Set
chopsticks, rest & placemat

Serve sushi - or any Asian dish - in style with a bead-trimmed mat and chopsticks.
The fanciful dragonfly's beaded body makes a colorful chopstick rest.

By Patty Cox

SUPPLIES

Woven wood or bamboo slat placemat
   with bound ends

Chopsticks

Round green beads, 10mm

1 round bead, 5mm

Green E beads

Green seed beads

Green bugle beads, 5mm

20 gauge gold wire

24 gauge gold wire

Triangular gold bead charm

Gold eyepin

Beading thread and needle

TOOLS

Needlenose pliers

Roundnose pliers

Drill and 1/16" drill bit

Wire cutters

INSTRUCTIONS FOR PLACEMAT

Using beading thread and needle, sew beads to make a fringe on the edges of the placemat: Thread each part with a 10mm bead and a seed bead, bring the thread around the seed bead and back through the 10mm bead. Knot thread on placemat edge. Cut thread. Space the beads evenly.

Continued on page 88

continued from page 86

INSTRUCTIONS FOR BEADED CHOPSTICKS

1. Drill 1/16" hole through the top of one chopstick.
2. Insert a headpin through the hole. Make a loop in the wire end with roundnose pliers.
3. Thread another headpin with:
   a seed bead
   an e bead
   a seed bead
   a 10mm bead
   a seed bead
   an e bead
   a seed bead
   Make a loop in the end with round-nose pliers.
4. Attach the two loops of the head-pins, making a beaded dangle.

INSTRUCTIONS FOR DRAGONFLY CHOPSTICK REST

1. Cut 1 yd. of 24 gauge wire. Thread wire center through triangle bead charm with the round 5mm bead in the center of charm. (Fig. 1)
2. Form one wing by threading 17 bugle beads with a seed bead between each bugle bead on the wire. Loop beaded wire back to center. Twist wires together. (Fig. 2)
3. Form a second wing on the same side with 17 bugles and seed beads. Loop beaded wire back to center. Twist wires together. Run wire tail through center hole to other side. (Fig. 3)

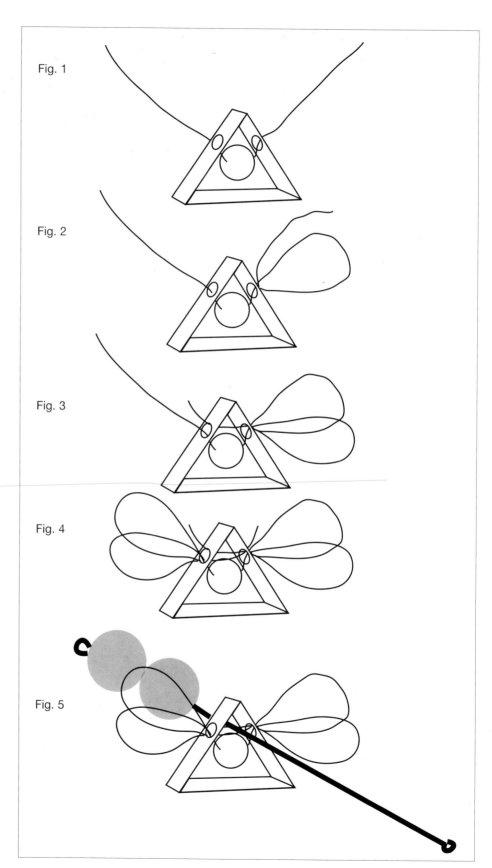

Fig. 1

Fig. 2

Fig. 3

Fig. 4

Fig. 5

4. Form two wings on the opposite side. Run wire tail through center hole to other side. (Fig. 4) Pull wire tails together and twist to tighten. Cut tails.

5. Cut 4" of 20 gauge wire. Loop one end with roundnose pliers. Thread two 10mm beads on the wire next to the loop. Thread wire through top of triangle charm over bead. Add 22 e beads to wire tail. Loop wire end with roundnose pliers. (Fig. 5) ❑

Cocktails, Anyone?
skewers & picks

Beaded skewers and picks are a festive way to serve party foods, and they make a delightful hostess gift. A martini-loving friend would adore a set of picks in the classic glass shape with the red and green beaded "olive."

By Patty Cox

SUPPLIES

16 gauge buss wire

24 gauge wrapping wire, silver or gold

Assorted beads, including an 8mm green bead, a 4mm red bead, and various 8mm beads with large holes

Headpins

Household cement

TOOLS

Roundnose pliers

Needlenose pliers

Nylon-jaw pliers

Jig with pegs (for martini glass pick)

Wire cutters

INSTRUCTIONS FOR MARTINI PICK

1. Cut 20" of buss wire. Arrange pegs in jig as in Fig. 4.
2. Thread an 8mm green bead and a 4mm red bead on the center of the buss wire. Place the center of buss wire (with beads) over the top two pegs.
3. Firmly pull wires around pegs, shaping a martini glass. Remove wire from jig.
4. Using nylon-jaw pliers, tighten the angles of the glass shape, using the photo as a guide.
5. Using roundnose pliers, form a loop in one wire tail at the bottom of martini glass. Cut tail.
6. Bend the other wire tail straight down under the martini glass.
7. Dot top wire with glass cement. Slide beads over glue. Let dry. ❏

INSTRUCTIONS FOR WRAPPED BEAD SKEWERS

1. Cut 6" of buss wire. Form a loop in one end with round-nose pliers.
2. Thread three large-hole 8mm beads on wire.
3. Cut 12" of 24 gauge wire. Thread wire through beads, making a 1" tail at skewer top. (Fig. 1)
4. Wrap the long tail tightly around the skewer wire at the bottom of beads, then continue spiraling 24 gauge wire around beads. Wrap end tightly around skewer wire. Cut tail. (Fig. 2)
5. *Option:* With needlenose pliers, grasp one wire wrap on bead. Twist needlenose to tighten wire and form a decorative bend in wire wrap. (Fig. 3)

INSTRUCTIONS FOR BEAD DANGLE SKEWERS OR PICKS

1. Cut 6" of buss wire. Form a loop in one end with round-nose pliers.
2. Thread beads on headpin. Trim end of headpin to 3/8" beyond beads. Form a loop in the end of the headpin with roundnose pliers.
3. Connect end loop of dangle to skewer loop.

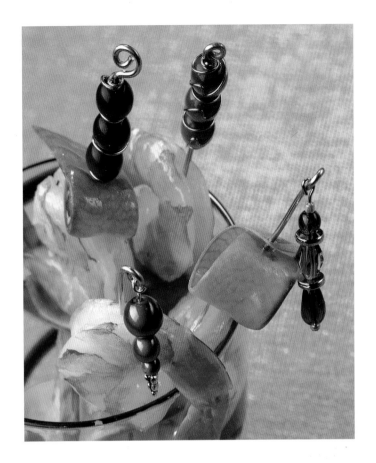

Fig. 1 - Wrapped beads, step 1.

Fig. 2 - Wrapped beads, step 2.

Fig. 3 - Wrapped beads, step 3.

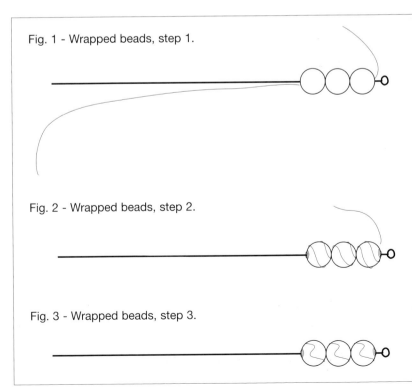

Fig. 4 - Peg placement on jig for Martini Pick

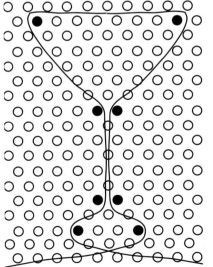

Between the Pages
bookmark

A thoughtful gift for book-loving friends, this flattened-wire bookmark shines
above the rest. It's quick and easy - why not make one for every member
of your reading group?

By Patty Cox

SUPPLIES

16 gauge aluminum wire

Silver headpin

Silver seed beads

Green round bead, 4mm

Turquoise bicone bead, 8mm

Blue teardrop bead, 9mm

TOOLS

Roundnose pliers

Hammer

Wire cutters

Brick

INSTRUCTIONS

1. Cut 15" of aluminum wire. Hold wire end with roundnose pliers. Form wire scroll according to pattern.
2. Using a hammer, flatten scroll on a hard surface, such as a brick.
3. Thread headpin with beads. Hold wire end with roundnose pliers. Form a loop in headpin end.
4. Thread loop on bookmark scroll. Tighten wire loop to secure beads in place. ❑

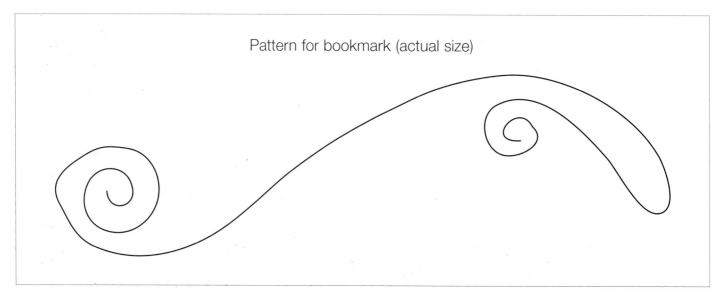

Pattern for bookmark (actual size)

Where's My Keys?
key ring dangle

Color code your keys and dress up a plain key ring with beaded dangles.

Any combination of beads, in any colors, will do.

By Barbara Mansfield

SUPPLIES

18 gauge silver wire

1 silver metal bead, 9mm

2 white beads, 9mm

2 turquoise beads, 9mm

1 lampwork bead, 12mm

1 silver bead, 6mm

1 green bead, 13mm

1 multi-green glass bead, 16mm

1 turquoise glass bead, 1"

TOOLS

Roundnose pliers

Wire cutters

INSTRUCTIONS

1. Cut 9" of wire and make loop on one end, using roundnose pliers.
2. String on the wire:
   the 9mm silver metal bead
   a 9mm turquoise bead
   the lampwork bead
   a 9mm turquoise bead
   the 6mm silver bead
   the 13mm green bead
   a 9mm white bead
   the 16mm multi-green glass bead
   a 9mm white bead
   the large turquoise glass bead
3. Make a swirl, using roundnose pliers, and cut off excess wire. ❏

Swaying in the Breeze
ceiling fan pull

Make beaded pulls in colors that coordinate with the colors of your rooms.

By Barbara Mansfield

SUPPLIES

18 gauge silver wire

2 blue glass beads, 15mm

1 clear glass oval bead, 13mm

2 blue flat beads, 9mm

2 silver spacer beads, 6mm

2 silver metal filler beads, 8mm

Ball chain with hook

TOOLS

Curling tool or 1/4" dowel

Roundnose pliers

Wire cutters

INSTRUCTIONS:

1. Cut 12" of wire and make a loop in the top as a stop for the beads and as a way to attach piece to chain.
2. String on wire the following beads:
   6mm silver metal filler bead
   15mm blue glass bead
   8mm silver metal filler bead
   15mm blue glass bead
   8mm silver metal filler bead
   blue flat bead
   clear glass oval bead
   blue flat bead
   6mm silver filler bead
3. Insert end of wire in curling tool and twist to make bottom curl; or wrap around dowel. Remove tool and pull wire to loosen.
4. Add ball chain to top. ❏

Greek Key
bookmark

You'll never lose your place with this beaded dangle bookmark. The black wire is thin enough to fit comfortably between the pages. The beaded dangle hangs below the book pages while the wire Greek Key design clips to page.

By Barbara Mansfield

SUPPLIES

18 gauge black wire

26 gauge silver wire

1 gray marble donut bead, 1"

1 black glass bead, 5/8"

1 clear bead, 8mm

3 black round beads, 8mm

4 flat silver beads, 10mm

5 charcoal spacer beads

2 bronze flat beads with center holes, 6mm

2 charcoal flat beads with side holes, 6mm

Crimp bead

TOOLS

Crimping pliers

Wire cutters

Roundnose pliers

INSTRUCTIONS

1. Cut 10" of 26 gauge silver wire. Bend wire in half and loop donut bead at center bend of wire.
2. On both wires, thread on:
   the black 5/8" glass bead
   the clear 8mm glass bead
   a charcoal spacer
   an 8mm black round bead
   a charcoal spacer
   3 flat silver beads
   a charcoal spacer
3. Split wires. To each wire, add:
   a flat 6mm charcoal bead
   a charcoal spacer
   an 8mm round black bead
4. Pull wires together. String on a 10mm flat silver bead and two bronze flat beads.
5. String on the crimp bead. Put end through crimp bead, leaving a loop. Crimp with tool.
6. Cut a piece of 18 gauge black wire that is longer than your book length + 8". I cut my wire to 18" for my 10" long book. Bend one end of the wire to make the Greek key design, using the pattern provided. Make a loop in the opposite end, using roundnose pliers.
7. Hook dangle on loop and tighten. ❏

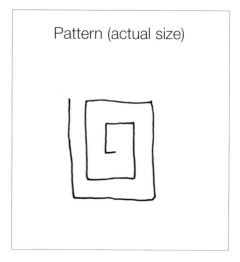

Pattern (actual size)

Cork It
bottle stoppers

You'll need six to seven beads for each stopper you make. This is a great way to display favorite beads and a quick and easy gift. Use them for flavored vinegars, oils, or spirits or as a stopper for bottles of bath salts or bubble bath.

By Dena Mansfield

SUPPLIES

For one stopper

18 gauge silver wire

Various glass beads, 5mm to 10mm

Assorted lampwork beads

A cork to fit your bottle

Strong multi-purpose adhesive

TOOLS

Roundnose pliers

Awl

Wire cutter

INSTRUCTIONS

For one stopper

1. Cut a 6" piece of wire. Bend wire into swirl about 3/4" diameter, using roundnose pliers.
2. Thread various beads on wire to make a section 1" to 1-1/2" long. Set aside.
3. Push awl into cork to make a hole. Apply adhesive to end of wire and insert in the hole in the cork. Let dry. ❏

Message on a Bottle

note holder

This cork bottle stopper could hold a menu, placecards at the table, instructions for a food gift, or reminders.

By Barbara Mansfield

SUPPLIES

18 gauge silver wire

9 assorted beads (I used silver and turquoise beads - flat ones and round ones - of various sizes.)

Cork to fit your bottle

Strong multi-purpose adhesive

TOOLS

Wire cutters

Roundnose pliers

Awl

INSTRUCTIONS

1. Cut a 10" piece of silver wire. Using roundnose pliers, make a swirl on one end of wire.
2. String beads on the wire, starting with the smallest bead and ending with the largest one. Set aside.
3. Push awl into cork to make a hole. Apply adhesive to end of wire and insert in the hole in the cork. Let dry. ❏

Cool Refreshments
drinks tub

A galvanized tub gets all dressed up for the party with colorful bead-and-wire dangles. Using pre-strung beads makes this a fast, easy project. But, of course, you can always string your own.

By Kathi Bailey

SUPPLIES

Aluminum wire, 24 gauge

Red crystal faceted beads, 8mm

Purple faceted beads, 8mm

Copper beads, 6mm

7 ft. pre-strung multi-color beads, 4mm

Gold metal cone beads

Assorted crystal beads and jewelry pieces

Galvanized oval tin tub, 36"

26 eyepins, 2"

TOOLS

Drill and drill bit

Needlenose pliers

Roundnose pliers

Wire cutters

Pencil

Measuring tape

INSTRUCTIONS

1. Measure, mark, and drill 13 holes on each side of the tub, spaced approximately 2-1/2" apart, as close to the top lip as possible.
2. Cut 26 pieces of wire, each 1-1/2" long. Use needlenose pliers to make loops. Insert a loop through each drilled hole.
3. String beads and jewelry on eyepins in various combinations to make dangles. Make a loop at the end of each dangle with roundnose pliers.
4. Attach each dangle to a wire loop at each drilled hole.
5. Attach one end of bead strand at a handle. Attach bead strands to wire loops, cutting small pieces of wire to attach. Allow slackness in the bead strand so that it loops from hole to hole. Take strand all around tub, cut off any excess. Attach other end at handle. ❑

A Is for Art
twig letters

Decorated with beads and wire, then formed into letters, twigs become an artful decorating accessory. Use branches pruned from your shrubbery or collected twigs to form letters of a word or your monogram. Cut branches at forks to make letters like R or A. Our letters are 18" tall. Choose bead colors to match your decor.

By Kathi Bailey

SUPPLIES

Red faceted crystal beads, 8mm
Purple faceted crystal beads, 8mm
White round beads, 6mm
Gold beads, 3mm
Red crystal beads, 10mm
Red seed beads, 10/0
Branches, twigs, or vines to form letters
24 gauge gold wire

TOOLS

Wire cutters
Pruning shears
Pencil

INSTRUCTIONS

1. Cut branches with pruning shears to make desired word or letters.
2. Form letters and secure at joints by wrapping with gold wire. Leave 12" wire tails for attaching beads.
3. String beads on wire tails, alternating colors.
4. Cut three to four additional 18" pieces of wire and attach at various points on twig letters.
5. String red seed beads on other wire pieces. Loop the seed bead strands around the letters. Curl the ends around a pencil to finish. ❏

Jeweled Furniture
table trim

A beaded apron is an unexpected touch on a traditional demi-lune table. Adding gold beads to the metal medallions at the tops of the legs continues the look.

By Kathi Bailey

SUPPLIES

Black bugle beads, #3

Red rocaille beads, size 10/0

White rocaille beads, size 10/0

Copper seed beads, size 10/0

Gold seed beads, size 10/0

Light aqua seed beads, size 10/0

Half-round wooden table with apron and leg medallions

80 grit sandpaper

Tracing paper

White transfer paper

White jewelry glue

Liquid clear matte sealer

TOOLS

Pencil

Foam brush

Stylus

INSTRUCTIONS

1. Lightly sand table apron so glue will adhere to the wood surface.
2. Using photos as a guide, create a geometric pattern to fit the table you wish to decorate. Transfer shapes to left side of apron. Reverse design and repeat on right side.
3. Create borders first by running a thin line of glue around edge of each shape. Place black bugle beads end to end in the glue to create the border. Let dry.
4. Working one shape at a time, fill in each shape with glue. Place seed or rocaille beads, using the photo as a guide for color placement. Let dry.
5. Brush beaded area *only* with clear matte sealer. Let dry. ❏

The World My Wilderness

VINCENT CANBY   LIVING QUARTERS

Pearls & Jewels
round tin box

A jeweled box can hold favorite jewelry on your dresser.

By Kathi Bailey

SUPPLIES

Green seed beads, size 10/0

Pearls, 6mm

Oval pearls, 1/2mm

Assorted crystal jewelry

Pre-strung multi-color round beads, 4mm

Round tin box, 3" diameter size (recycled)

White spray primer

Metallic gold spray paint

White jewelry glue

Matte sealer spray

Gold braid, 10"

TOOLS

Tweezers

foam brush

INSTRUCTIONS

1. Spray entire tin with two coats of white primer. Let dry.
2. Spray with gold paint. Let dry.
3. Apply glue to sides and edges of lid, spreading glue evenly with brush. You will need a thick coat.
4. Press rows of pre-strung round beads in the glue, using the photo as a guide.
5. Apply a bead of glue around edge of box top.
6. Glue a row of pearls inside the round beads on box top. Tweezers will help with placement.
7. Arrange crystal jewelry and pearl(s) at center of lid. Glue in place. Let dry.
8. Fill in open areas with glue. Press green seed beads over glue to cover. Let dry.
9. Spray with matte sealer. Let dry.
10. Glue gold braid around the sides of the tin base. Let dry. ❏

Flowers & Leaves
heart-shaped tin box

Beaded boxes are fun storage for all kinds of items.

By Kathi Bailey

SUPPLIES

Purple bugle beads, #3

Blue rocaille beads, size 10/0

3 blue goldstone beads, 6mm

Flat gold leaf charms

Heart tin, 5" (recycled box)

White spray primer

Metallic gold spray paint

White jewelry glue

Matte sealer spray

TOOLS

Tweezers

Foam brush

INSTRUCTIONS

1. Spray entire tin with two coats white primer. Let dry.
2. Spray with gold paint. Let dry.
3. Apply a thick coat of glue to sides and top edges of lid. Use foam brush to spread glue evenly. Press bugle beads in glue to cover the sides of the lid and make a border around the outer edge. Use tweezers to help with placment.
4. Place leaves as shown in the photo. Glue in place.
5. Add goldstone beads on top of the clusters of three leaves. Let dry.
6. Fill open areas with a mix of blue rocaille beads and bugle beads. Let dry.
7. Spray with matte sealer. Let dry. ❏

Tiny Treasure
rectangular tin box

Bugle beads, laid end-to-end on the outer edge of the lid and upright around the sides, make a colorful border for a tin box.

By Kathi Bailey

SUPPLIES

Orange bugle beads, #2
Copper seed beads, size 10/0
Gold seed beads, size 10/0
Pearls, 2mm
1 pearl, 8mm
Assorted costume jewelry
Rectangular tin, 3-1/2" x 2-1/2"
  (recycled mint box)
White spray primer
Metallic gold spray paint
White jewelry glue
Matte sealer spray

TOOLS

Tweezers
Foam brush

INSTRUCTIONS

1. Spray entire tin with two coats white primer. Let dry.
2. Spray with gold paint. Let dry.
3. Apply glue to sides and top edges of lid. Press three rows of bugle beads to sides and three rows on top edges to make a border. Let dry.
4. Arrange jewelry and pearls inside the bugle bead border. Glue in place. Let dry.
5. Spread glue in open areas. Fill with copper and gold seed beads. Let dry. ❏

Colors of the Sea
fish bowl trim & base

Instructions begin on page 110.

Colors of the Sea
fish bowl trim & base

Colors of the seas and sand are used to trim a plain glass fish bowl.

By Kathi Bailey

SUPPLIES FOR FISH BOWL TRIM

Blue pebble seed beads, size 6/0

Blue seed beads, size 10/0

Frosted white faceted beads, 4mm

Frosted white round beads, 6mm

Clear crystal beads, 10mm

Round glass fish bowl, 6" diameter

Pearl cotton thread

TOOLS

Tweezers

Beading needle

INSTRUCTIONS

Adjust measurements and number of beads if you are using a larger or smaller bowl.

1. Cut 24" of pearl cotton thread. Thread onto needle. Leave a 2" tail and string on:
   1 clear 10mm crystal bead
   1 white 4mm bead
   5 blue 6/0 seed beads
   1 white 6mm bead
   5 blue 6/0 seed beads
   1 white 4mm bead
   Repeat sequence seven (or more) times to make a strand to fit around the top of the bowl under the lip. Tie ends loosely. This is your base strand. Wait until the rest of the beading is completed to knot off and tie tightly.

2. Cut 60" pearl cotton and thread onto needle. Insert one end through one 10mm crystal bead, then through the 4mm bead, (beads that are strung on base strand) and pull through.

3. Add 1 blue 6/0 seed bead and 1 white 4mm bead. Repeat 4 more times.

4. Add 1 crystal 10mm bead and 1 white 4mm bead.

5. Add 15 blue seed beads and 1 frosted 6mm bead. Loop thread around round bead and run back up through the seed beads and the white 4mm bead, and the crystal bead.

6. Repeat step 3.

7. Then run the thread through the 4mm bead, the crystal bead, and the other 4mm bead on the base strand.

8. Repeat steps 3 through 7 until you reach the starting point.

9. Knot tightly including the base strand, to secure. Trim ends.

10. Slip over top of glass bowl. ❏

SUPPLIES FOR FISH BOWL BASE

Gold seed beads, size 10/0

Light blue seed beads, size 10/0

Medium blue seed beads, size 10/0

Dark blue seed beads, size 10/0

White seed beads, size 10/0

Oval pearls, 1/2mm

Round unfinished wooden box with lid, 5" diameter

Acrylic craft paints - Cappuccino, Coastal Blue

White jewelry glue

Matte sealer spray

Sandpaper

TOOLS

Pencil

Foam brush

INSTRUCTIONS

1. Paint box base with two coats Coastal Blue. Let dry and sand between coats.

2. Paint lid with two coats Cappuccino. Let dry and sand between coats.

3. Apply glue to edge of top of lid. Adhere one row of oval pearls around the entire edge. Let dry.

4. Divide sides of the box base with penciled wavy lines, to make three sections.

5. Working one section or area at a time, apply glue. Press light blue, medium blue, and dark blue seed beads in alternating sections to create "waves" around the base. Add some white beads at top to simulate the wave crest. Let dry.

6. Spray with matte sealer. Let dry.

7. Place fish bowl on base. ❏

Pretty as a Picture
beaded frame

A plain wooden picture frame is decorated with bead flowers and wire stems and leaves, which add dimensional appeal. Choose a paint color that matches the bead color you use for the background. Ours is light green.

By Kathi Bailey

SUPPLIES

18 gauge natural copper wire

18 gauge brown copper wire

White seed beads, size 10/0

Blue seed beads, size 10/0

Green seed beads, size 10/0

Purple bugle beads, #2

Unfinished wooden picture frame, 8" x 10"

Acrylic craft paint - Light Green

White jewelry glue

Tracing paper

Transfer paper

Matte sealer spray

TOOLS

Wire cutters

Needlenose pliers

Foam brush

Sandpaper

Stylus

INSTRUCTIONS

1. Paint entire frame with two coats Light Green. Let dry and sand between coats.
2. Trace pattern from book onto tracing paper. Transfer pattern to front of frame using a stylus.
3. Cut four lengths of copper wire, 12" each. Lay on base pattern and bend to create stems and leaves. Use needlenose pliers to make curlicues at the ends.
4. Make leaves from wire leaf pattern and attach to stems by wrapping with brown copper wire.
5. Put glue on frame along the base pattern lines and adhere wire shape to frame. Let dry.
6. Cut three 5" lengths of copper wire. Use needlenose pliers to create swirls for the center of each flower.
7. Fill flower centers with glue. Press swirls in glue. Add white seed beads to surround swirls.
8. Working one at a time, fill flower petals and shapes of beaded leaves with glue. Fill with seed beads, using the photo as a guide for color placement. Let dry.
9. Spray with matte sealer. Let dry. ❏

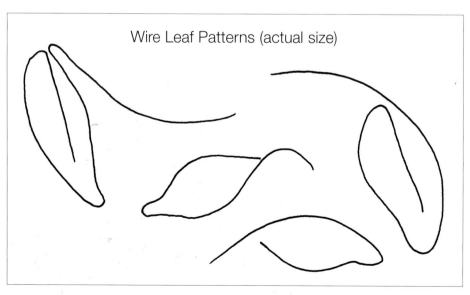

Wire Leaf Patterns (actual size)

See base pattern on page 114.

Pattern for Frame Base
(actual size)

Leafy Glow
trimmed candle holder

Leaf-shaped glass beads, beaded "vines," and wire tendrils decorate a painted wooden candlestick.

By Kathi Bailey

SUPPLIES

24 gauge gold wire

Leaf-shaped glass beads

Gold rose metal beads, 9mm

Gold round metal beads, 4mm

Green seed beads

Unfinished wooden candle holder

Acrylic craft paints - Pure Gold, Aqua

Sandpaper

Liquid clear matte sealer

TOOLS

Wire cutters

Needlenose pliers

Foam brush

Pencil

INSTRUCTIONS

Paint:

1. Paint entire candlestick with two coats Aqua. Let dry and sand between coats.
2. Trim with Pure Gold, using the photo as a guide for color placement. Let dry.
3. Brush with clear matte sealer. Let dry.

Decorate:

1. Cut four 24" pieces of gold wire.
2. String green seed beads on one piece of wire. Loop ends to secure. Wrap the beaded wire around the candlestick, using the photo as a guide.
3. Wrap the center of one piece of wire around the candlestick two to three times, keeping the ends free and separate. Add leaf beads and gold rose beads to wires, using the photo as a guide. Finish with a leaf bead. Trim the end of the wire, leaving a short tail. Using needlenose pliers to bend the wire to make a small loop, and pass the tail through the hole in the bead.
4. Repeat with remaining wire pieces and beads.
5. To make tendrils, wrap wire pieces around the candlestick. Coil the ends with pliers or wrap around a pencil to make a spiral. ❏

Bead Mosaics

These bead mosaics use dimensional paint to adhere closely spaced beads to a surface to create a design. There are two techniques for arranging the beads - in one, the beads are placed one by one (the "loose bead" method); in the other, the beads are strung on thread and laid in place (the "strung bead" method). Two bead mosaic suncatcher projects follow the Basic Instructions.

By Cindy Gorder

Basic Instructions for Bead Mosaics

SUPPLIES

Seed beads

Dimensional paint, clear or color of beads

A surface (Here, we're using a glass shape.)

TOOLS

Straight pins *or* beading needle and thread

Paper towels

Felt square or bead board

BASIC TECHNIQUE

1. Place pattern beneath glass shape.
2. Squeeze out paint in lines, following pattern.
3. Place beads in paint, using either the Loose Bead Method *or* the Strung Bead Method. (See below.) Let dry.

The Loose Bead Method:
Pick up one or more beads on a straight pin. Position the beads in the paint with the holes of the beads facing sideways, *not up*. Hold the bead-loaded pin horizontally just above (but not touching) the paint line. Slightly tilt the end of the pin toward the paint and let the beads slide off. Use your index finger to push and guide them into a tightly packed row in the paint. Use the end of the

pin to arrange and nudge beads close together in the paint. Keep your pin tool clean by wiping it often with a paper towel. Paint buildup on the pin tip makes it difficult to pick up and place the beads.

The Strung Bead Method:
String beads on thread. Remove needle. Holding ends of thread, lay closely packed beads in paint. Nudge beads in place, then carefully pull out the thread. Nudge beads back into position if they shift while you remove the string.

TIPS

- Hold the surface at an angle that allows you best access to the area you want to apply beads.

- Make sure your workspace has good lighting. For a better view, try wearing reading glasses or using a magnifying device.

- Use a square of felt, a bead board with grooves, or some of the shallow dishes sold in bead shops and bead departments of crafts stores to hold beads as you work.

- The paint sets up fairly quickly so it's a good idea to work on several small areas at a time, making sure not to disturb any recently positioned beads. Reapply paint as needed. You will soon get a sense of how much paint you can work before it begins to harden. Place beads one at a time on hard-to-reach areas. Place several beads at one time on easy-to-reach areas.

- Work different areas of your overall design to allow recently placed beads to set up undisturbed. When necessary, stop working to allow the paint to harden before continuing.

- When the paint has hardened (this can take several minutes to an hour), you can work in adjacent areas without disturbing the set beads.

- If the paint dries before you have applied the beads, you can apply more paint. If it seems too thick, carefully scrape off the dried paint before applying more.

- Fill small gaps with additional dimensional paint.

- Keep the applicator tip of your paint container clean. Use an extra pin as a stopper to save constant opening and closing as you work.

- Avoid rough handling of your finished beadwork. Save a few beads for quick repairs. If beads fall off, simply apply more paint and replace missing beads.

- Don't worry if there is excess paint around the beads. When it dries, it will blend in with the beads and enhance the overall look. If you wish, use a craft knife to slice through excess dried paint next to the beadwork, then carefully peel away the paint you don't want.

Mosaic Star
suncatcher

By Cindy Gorder

SUPPLIES

Dimensional paint - Ice Sparkle

Star-shaped glass blank with pre-drilled hole for hanging

Two shades of green seed beads, size 15

Copper wire (for hanger)

Glass cleaner and paper towels

TOOLS

Wire cutters

Pattern (actual size)

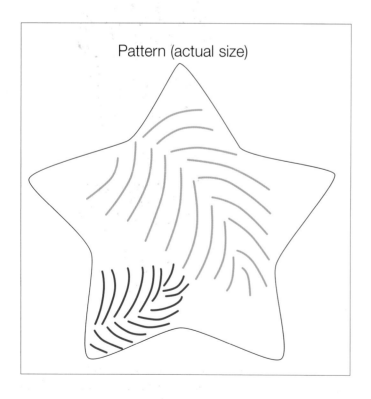

INSTRUCTIONS

See the Basic Instructions for Bead Mosaics on the previous pages.

1. Clean the suncatcher with glass cleaner.
2. Place glass shape over pattern and apply fabric paint on a few of the pattern lines. Apply seed beads into the wet paint, using the photo as a guide for color placement. Continue applying paint and beads until the pattern is complete. Let dry completely.
3. Thread wire though hole. Make a loop for hanging and twist to secure. ❏

Oval Flower
suncatcher

By Cindy Gorder

SUPPLIES

Dimensional paint - Ice Sparkle

Oval glass blank with pre-drilled hole for hanging

Two shades of green seed beads, size 15

Lilac seed beads, size 15

Green sheer ribbon (for hanger)

Glass cleaner and paper towels

TOOLS

Scissors

INSTRUCTIONS

See the Basic Instructions for Bead Mosaics on the previous pages.

1. Clean the suncatcher with glass cleaner.
2. Place glass shape over pattern and apply dimensional paint on a few of the pattern lines. Apply seed beads into the wet paint, using the photo as a guide for color placement. Outline shapes first, then fill in next to outlines and work toward the center. Continue applying paint and beads until the pattern is complete. Let dry completely.
3. Thread ribbon though hole. Tie to make a loop for hanging. Trim ends of ribbon with scissors. ❑

Pattern (actual size)

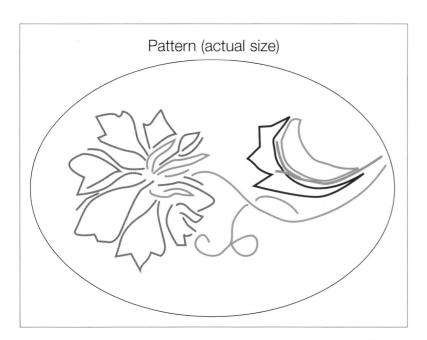

Art Deco Inspiration
journal

The angular lines of Art Deco inspired the cover design of this journal. Shimmering beads in coordinating colors were used to decorate the title page. You can use a journal of any size for this project by adjusting the size of the pattern.

By Cindy Gorder

SUPPLIES

Dimensional paint - Peacock Sparkle, Violet Sparkle

Three shades of blue bugle beads - light, medium, dark, 4mm (10 grams of each color)

Twisted purple bugle beads, 7mm (12 grams)

Black bugle beads (5 grams)

Pre-strung black seed beads, size 11 (one hank)

Pre-strung yellow-green seed beads, size 11 (two hanks)

Pre-strung blue-green seed beads, size 11 (two strands)

Loose *or* pre-strung purple seed beads, size 11

Loose *or* pre-strung iris-blue seed beads, size 11

Blue flat-back round cabochon, 6mm

2 blue flat-back square cabochons, 9mm

Journal, 6-1/4" x 8-1/2"

Mat board, 5-1/2" x 7-3/4"

Heavy-duty double-sided adhesive, 5-1/2" x 7-3/4"

Card stock, 5-1/2" x 7-5/8"

Stamp pad - Purple

Small pieces of decorative papers

Gold leafing pen

Self-adhesive mounting squares

Hole punch

Tracing paper

Transfer paper

TOOLS

Rubber stamps - "Journal," peacock feather

Markers *or* colored pencils - Deep blue, medium blue, light blue, purple

Stylus

INSTRUCTIONS

See the Basic Instructions for Bead Mosaics.

Prepare Cover:

1. Trace pattern from book onto tracing paper. Transfer pattern to mat board.
2. Fill in transferred pattern with four different marker or pencil colors that correspond with the four bugle bead colors used in the design (Fig. 1).

Apply Design on Cover:

The dimensional paint is the glue that holds the beads. A section at a time of dimensional paint is applied to surface and beads are placed.

1. Squeeze out a line of peacock dimensional paint and apply the light blue bugle beads along the paint line, nudging them close together. (Fig. 2) Tap lightly to ensure they are making solid contact with the paint and mat board. Where another bead color will intersect, leave a gap to accommodate those beads.
2. After all the light blue beads are attached, outline them with black seed beads, applying the paint first as the glue. (Fig. 3 on page 123)
3. Lay in the medium blue bugle beads.

Continued on page 122

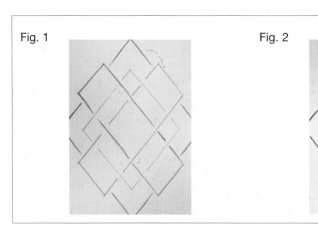

Fig. 1

Fig. 2

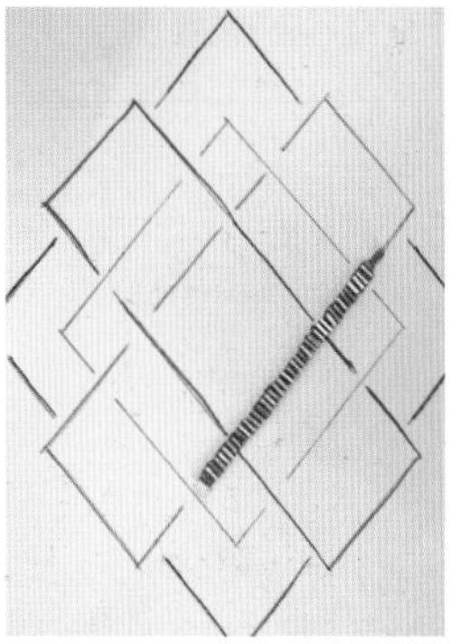

Art Deco Inspiration
continued from page 120

4. Outline with black seed beads (Fig. 4 on page 123).
5. Lay in the dark blue bugle beads.
6. Outline with black seed beads.
7. Lay in the purple bugle beads.
8. Outline with black seed beads. (Fig. 5 on page 123)

Apply Background on Cover:
Fill in the remaining areas with yellow-green seed beads, starting with outer row within a section and working toward the center of the section. Use the photo as a guide for placement. Before filling in the center diamond, glue square cabochons in place, then bead around them. Let completed beading set overnight.

Assemble Cover:
1. Cover the back of the beaded mat board with heavy-duty double sided adhesive and adhere to front cover of journal.
2. Outline edges of mat board with peacock dimensional paint applied to journal cover next to mat board. Apply black bugle beads over the paint outline to finish edges of mat board.
3. Apply additional paint as needed to fill any gaps.

Decorate Title Page:
1. Stamp or hand-letter "Journal" on a small piece of decorative paper.
2. Cover lines, one letter at a time, with violet dimensional paint and apply purple seed beads.
3. When the paint is completely set, trim and edge the title plate with the gold leafing pen.
4. Mount the beaded title plate on a torn rectangle of a second decorative paper. Set aside.
5. Punch the card stock to fit the rings

of the journal.
6. Stamp or draw a peacock feather on the lower right corner of the card stock.
7. Using violet dimensional paint, glue the round cabochon in place for the "eye" and allow glue to set.
8. Using peacock dimensional paint, glue iris-blue seed beads around the cabochon and glue blue-green seeds to create the feather. Fill in large gaps with peacock dimensional paint. Let set up overnight.
9. Use mounting squares to attach the title plate to the card stock.
10. Insert title page in journal. ❏

Pattern for Art Deco Inspiration Journal Cover

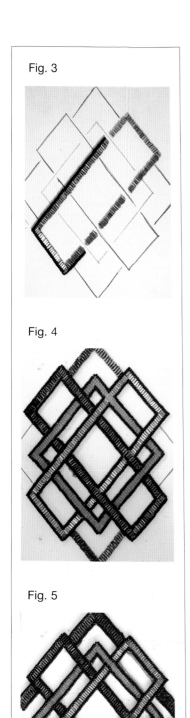

Fig. 3

Fig. 4

Fig. 5

Love Light
Candle Trim

These candles are studded with beads, butterflies and a beautiful stamped polymer clay piece. If you choose to light the candle, once it has burned down to create a well, a votive candle or tea light can be inserted into well and burned so that large candle can stay intact.

By Lisa Galvin

SUPPLIES

2 off white 3" pillar candles

2 ounce block of gold soft polymer clay

6" x 12" piece of brass 18 gauge metal mesh

Browning Poem rubber stamp

"Greetings" rubber stamp set

36" length copper wired edge ribbon, 2-1/2" wide

Antique gold dragonfly charm

Gold earring backs from post-type earring findings

Four 1" gold head pins

10-12 gold eyepins (pins with looped end)

7mm gold jump rings

Amber glass teardrop beads

Fiberfil quilt batting

TOOLS

*Pasta machine (or acrylic clay roller)

*Two small glass recycled mayonnaise jars

*Miniature heart shaped cookie cutter (or craft knife to cut your own heart shapes)

*Baking sheet

Home oven

Jewelry pliers

Wire cutters

Toothpick

Scissors

Tools used for polymer clay should not be used again with food and should be dedicated to use with polymer clay.

INSTRUCTIONS

Polymer Clay Piece:

1. Preheat oven to 265 degrees. Knead gold clay to condition.

2. Roll it or send through pasta machine to create a sheet that is approximately 3/16" thick. Rubber stamp the sheet with Browning poem stamp; gently pressing the stamp pattern into the soft clay. Cut five heart shapes from outer edges and set aside. Tear away remaining sheet to create a rough-edged wrap for candle. Size shown here measures approximately 3 1/2" x 4-1/2". Place glass jar on its side. Place piece over a glass jar for baking. Set aside.

3. Knead excess clay for use in creating second candle wrap. Roll four to five times through pasta machine to eliminate any trapped air pockets. Make a sheet 3/16" thick. Stamp the piece randomly with word rubber stamps. Tear edges to create a similar size clay wrap. Place piece over second mayonnaise jar. Lightly press heart shaped pieces onto top of clay wrap as shown.

4. Use a toothpick to make small holes randomly in both clay wraps. These will be used to add beaded accents that attach clay piece to candle later. Refer to photo for placement.

5. Place fiberfil quilt batting onto baking sheet. Position jars on their back side on fiberfil, with polymer clay pieces facing upward. Nestle jars slightly (if needed) into fiberfil to prevent them from rolling during baking or when moving tray. Bake as directed by manufacturer or at 265 degrees for 30 minutes. Remove from oven and let cool. Remove clay from jars.

Decorate Candle:

1. Wrap bottom of each candle with a length of ribbon and tie an overhand knot. To prevent raveling trim ribbon ends to form a "V" shape using scissors.

2. Cut a piece of brass mesh to fit behind each clay wrap, curling or curving edges to add interest.

3. Use wire cutters to trim eye pins to 3/4". Do not trim away the looped end.

4. Attach wrap to candle by positioning as desired over brass mesh. Insert eye pins through an earring back, then through holes made in clay. Additional eye pins can be inserted into candle only, scattering a few around edges of wrap to accent.

5. Open jump rings, slide on an amber teardrop bead. Hang from looped end of eye pins and close ring to hold in place, allowing bead to dangle from the eye pin.

6. Attach dragonfly to candle using 4 head pins that have been trimmed to 3/4" long and inserted close to body. ❑

Seaside Dining
nautical stemware

Add an artistic touch to inexpensive stemware with wire and beads.
Hand wash decorated stemware and dry immediately after washing.

By Lisa Galvin

SUPPLIES

(For each glass)

8" length 18 gauge green wire

30" length 24 gauge silver wire

Stemmed wine or water glass

Acrylic pearlized beads:

- five 9 x 6mm dark blue oat shaped beads
- two green oat shaped beads
- five 4mm dark blue round beads
- one 6mm round gray bead

Small sea shell

TOOLS

Drill

5/32" Drill bit

Hot glue gun with clear glue stick

Scissors

Wooden skewer (or 1/8" dowel rod)

Wire cutters

INSTRUCTIONS

Beaded Flower:

1. Slide a 6mm round gray bead to center of a 20" length of silver wire. Twist wire twice to hold bead in place. *(See Fig. 1.)*
2. Insert one wire end through a dark blue oat shaped bead and a 4mm round bead so that they are positioned close to base of gray bead.

Bring wire end around 4mm round bead and back through oat shaped bead only. Gently pull wire until 4mm dark blue round bead is firmly locked into position at tip of oat bead. Twist wire at base of oat bead before continuing. *(See Fig. 2.)*

3. Repeat Step 2 to create four more "flower petals" that surround the gray center. Remember to twist the wire at base of each petal before continuing to next petal.

4. Once back at starting point, twist wire together three to four times at base of the flower. Cut off excess wire.

5. Leaves. Using remaining 10" length of silver wire, slide a green oat shaped bead onto remaining length, pushing it to center. Wrap one wire end around bead and twist once with opposite wire end; going just below bead to secure it in position. *(See Fig. 3.)* Slip on another green bead and repeat to finish leaves.

6. Wrap one end of green wire around wooden skewer four to six times to curl wire. Remove from skewer. Slide the flower onto the wire up to the curled loops. Silver wire can be wrapped two to three times around the green wire to hold in place (if needed). Trim excess silver wire from flower only. The green wire will be the stem of the flower with the curl at top of flower.

Trimming Glass:
1. Drill a small hole in top of seashell.
2. Position flower with green "stem" above seashell to determine desired "stem" length. Trim excess wire (if needed). Add a drop of hot glue to green wire end and insert into sea shell so that flower appears to be growing out of it.
3. Position beaded leaves at base of stem, just above seashell. Wrap the silver wire from leaves around the green stem wire to attach flower, leaves and seashell to glass stem. Trim excess wire. A small drop of hot glue may be applied to hold flower and seashell in desired upright position. ❑

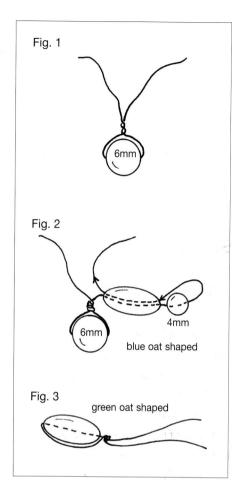

Fig. 1
6mm

Fig. 2
6mm
4mm
blue oat shaped

Fig. 3
green oat shaped

Metric Conversion Chart

Inches to Millimeters and Centimeters

Inches	MM	CM	Inches	MM	CM
1/8	3	.3	2	51	5.1
1/4	6	.6	3	76	7.6
3/8	10	1.0	4	102	10.2
1/2	13	1.3	5	127	12.7
5/8	16	1.6	6	152	15.2
3/4	19	1.9	7	178	17.8
7/8	22	2.2	8	203	20.3
1	25	2.5	9	229	22.9
1-1/4	32	3.2	10	254	25.4
1-1/2	38	3.8	11	279	27.9
1-3/4	44	4.4	12	305	30.5

Yards to Meters

Yards	Meters	Yards	Meters
1/8	.11	3	2.74
1/4	.23	4	3.66
3/8	.34	5	4.57
1/2	.46	6	5.49
5/8	.57	7	6.40
3/4	.69	8	7.32
7/8	.80	9	8.23
1	.91	10	9.14
2	1.83		

Index